THE SPIRIT OF CHRISTMAS

CREATIVE HOLIDAY IDEAS
BOOK EIGHTEEN

Christmas is a time to reflect on blessings, remember friends, and share joyful moments with family. To help make this holiday your best and brightest ever, we've gathered dozens of easy creative ideas and placed them in this volume. You'll find a Yuletide theme that's just right for your home, whether you prefer the beauty of golden stars, the serenity of a wintry forest, or the childhood whimsy of Santa Claus. Choose from a bounty of unique gifts to create, as well as thoughtful ways to present them. You'll also find a wide selection of recipes that will elicit exclamations of delight for their festive appearance and scrumptious flavor. This year, make your Christmas everything your heart desires.

LEISURE ARTS, INC.
Little Rock, Arkansas

THE SPIRIT OF CHRISTMAS
BOOK EIGHTEEN

EDITORIAL STAFF

Vice President and Editor-in-Chief: Sandra Graham Case
Executive Director of Publications: Cheryl Nodine Gunnells
Senior Director of Publications: Susan White Sullivan
Director of Designer Relations: Debra Nettles
Publications Director: Kristine Anderson Mertes
Design Director: Cyndi Hansen
Editorial Director: Susan Frantz Wiles
Senior Director of Public Relations and Retail Marketing: Stephen Wilson
Art Operations Director: Jeff Curtis

DESIGN

Design Manager: Diana Sanders Cates
Designers: Cherece Athy, Tonya Bradford Bates, Polly Tullis Browning, Peggy Elliott Cunningham, Anne Pulliam Stocks, Linda Diehl Tiano, Becky Werle, Lori Wenger, and Kim Kern

FOODS

Foods Editor: Celia Fahr Harkey, R.D.
Foods Associate Editor: Laura Siar Holyfield

OXMOOR HOUSE

Editor-in-Chief: Nancy Fitzpatrick Wyatt
Executive Editor: Susan Carlisle Payne
Foods Editors: Holley Contri Johnson, M.S., R.D. and Kelly Hooper Troiano
Photographers: Jim Bathie and Brit Huckabay
Photography Stylist: Ashley J. Wyatt
Contributing Photography Stylist: Missy Crawford
Test Kitchens Director: Elizabeth Tyler Luckett
Test Kitchens Assistant Director and Recipe Coordinator: Julie Christopher
Test Kitchens Staff: Kristi Carter, Nicole L. Faber, Tamara Goldis, Kathleen Royal Phillips, Jan A. Smith, Elise Weiss, and Kelley Self Wilton

TECHNICAL

Technical Editor: Leslie Schick Gorrell
Senior Technical Writer: Shawnna B. Bowles
Technical Writer: Theresa Hicks Young
Technical Associates: Susan Ackerman Carter and Cathy Hardy

EDITORIAL

Senior Editors: Linda L. Garner and Susan McManus Johnson
Associate Editor: Kimberly L. Ross

ART

Art Publications Director: Rhonda Hodge Shelby
Art Imaging Director: Mark Hawkins
Art Category Manager: Lora Puls
Senior Publications Designer: Dana Vaughn
Graphic Artists: Chad Brown, Amy Gerke, and Mandy Hickman
Imaging Technician: Mark R. Potter
Photographer: Russell Ganser
Photography Stylists: Janna Laughlin, Christy Myers, and Cassie Newsome
Publishing Systems Administrator: Becky Riddle
Publishing Systems Assistants: Clint Hanson, John P. Rose, and Chris Wertenberger

BUSINESS STAFF

Publisher: Rick Barton
Vice President, Finance: Tom Siebenmorgen
Director of Corporate Planning and Development: Laticia Mull Dittrich
Vice President, Retail Marketing: Bob Humphrey
Vice President, Sales: Ray Shelgosh
Vice President, National Accounts: Pam Stebbins
Director of Sales and Services: Margaret Reinold
Vice President, Operations: Jim Dittrich
Comptroller, Operations: Rob Thieme
Retail Customer Service Managers: Sharon Hall and Stan Raynor
Print Production Manager: Fred F. Pruss

"... and it was always said of him, that he knew how to keep Christmas well, if any man alive possessed the knowledge. May that be truly said of us, and all of us!"
— From *A Christmas Carol* by Charles Dickens

Library of Congress Catalog Card Number 98-65188
Hardcover ISBN 1-57486-321-5
Softcover ISBN 1-57486-322-3

10 9 8 7 6 5 4 3 2 1

CONTENTS
The *Sights* of Christmas

The *Sharing* of Christmas

The *Tastes* of Christmas

The *Tastes* of Christmas continued

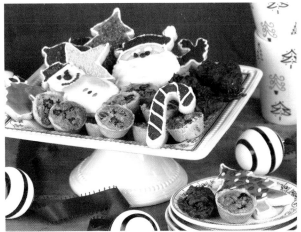

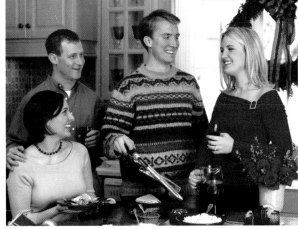

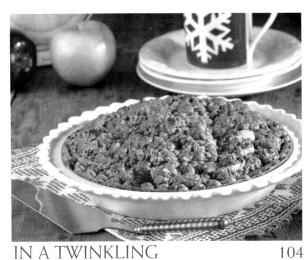

The Sights

# of Christmas

When you think about
Christmas, do you imagine
evergreen boughs filled with
lights and color? Do you see
stockings overflowing with
treasures or a table beautifully
set for a feast? This collection
of trees, tablescapes, and mantel
décor also includes a few quick
and easy creations, giving you
more time to observe the best
sights of the season ... the smiling
faces of your loved ones!

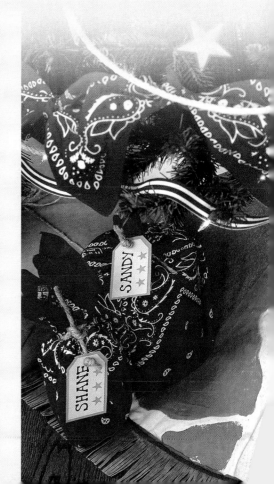

radiant STARS

Fill your holiday with an abundance of handmade stars and radiant red trimmings. With the many thousands of bead styles and bead trims available to you, these beautiful designs will reflect your originality — and that makes them perfect for gift-giving, as well as for decorating. This year, let Christmas joy shine with dazzling beads and the season's happiest hue.

The soft glow of candlelight creates a romantic balance to the vivacious red fabric spilling across an accent table. The **Bead-Trimmed Candlesticks** hold their tapers in grand style, and it's easy to add gold beads to the cut-glass globes for more sparkle. Red glass ball ornaments heap up in a crystal compote for an instant, dazzling centerpiece. Winding 'round it all, evergreen and bead garlands intertwine with gold ribbon, while ornaments of green and gold sparkle among the needles. Add beautiful bows to your packages this year, and delight the recipients by attaching handmade ornaments: our **Beaded Star**, **Chenille Tassel**, or **Stamped Mirror**.

This very special tree will have you seeing stars … and mirrors and tassels! In addition to the beaded ornaments used on the packages (*opposite*), the charming evergreen wears **Chenille Tassels**, **Gold Beaded Tassles**, and a variety of **Beaded Stars**. Traditional glass ornaments and garlands of ribbon and cord continue the dazzling theme. And the crowning glory is a **Beaded Star** made into a tree topper (*shown on page 9*) with the simple addition of a coiled wire threaded through the center of the star. The shine goes on to include a **Metal Stand**, the perfect foil for all the sparkle and glitter of our red-and-gold tree.

Instructions for Radiant Stars begin on page 116.

Dangle Beaded Stars from ribbon to create a magical garland. And let Beaded Votive Holders reflect candlelight from hundreds of tiny facets. The Christmas Angel (*opposite*) is the ultimate centerpiece for this most festive of celebrations. Graceful fabric wings spread behind her glorious beaded dress, while a gleaming brass candlestick holds the sweet seraphim upright. Her smooth, golden face gets its shape from an overturned glass vase.

Instructions for Radiant Stars begin on page 116.

christmas
is for
children

To children, Christmas is everything happy and good, all rolled into one special day. These craft foam creations for the play room are a child's idea of holiday fun.

Typical Christmas decorations are often off-limits to the youngest members of the household. But you can let little fingers explore craft foam creations without fearing the hazards of glass and tinsel. Craft foam is available in sheets and a myriad of pre-cut shapes, so making these jolly items will be just as fun for you.

Instructions for Christmas is for Children begin on page 124.

What a merry sight for children to see — Santa's left his hats and other whimsical shapes on a **Craft Foam Christmas Tree!** Circling the tree is an easy-to-make **Craft Foam Garland.** As well as the **Santa Hat Ornaments,** there are multi-color **Top Ornaments,** bouncy **Spiral Ornaments,** and frosty white **Snowflake Ornaments** *(close-up on page 14)*.

All aboard! Santa's Train is ready to take young imaginations on a Christmas adventure. Wooden crates, covered in craft foam, become a sturdy and colorful choo-choo. And the roomy box cars *(shown on page 15)* can store playthings year-round. A Whimsical Foam Stocking, with bobbing circles and tops, is a quick way to brighten a wall or door.

Waiting for Christmas can be a fun game with Countdown Santa! The jolly old elf loans his famous white beard so kiddies can remove one piece of candy each day until December 24. The pre-cut numbers on the pockets make this foam fellow easy to assemble, and just a touch of paint is needed for his cheeks.

Instructions for Christmas is for Children begin on page 124.

a
splendid
evening

For a holiday party with unique style, treat guests to the breathtaking elegance of decorations in lavender and silver, then serve a variety of extraordinary foods. The joy you create will give you and your friends many fond memories to cherish.

A buffet glows with festive beauty when it features a **Beaded Candlescape**. And from the Lavender Tree Topper to the drifts of shantung and sheer fabrics below, the tree *(opposite)* dazzles with **Pillow Ornaments** and Beaded Wire Ornaments. **Beaded Bows,** faux fern greenery, purple ribbon, silver bead garland, and matte glass balls also adorn the boughs.

Instructions and recipes for A Splendid Evening begin on page 128.

Our **Lavender Centerpiece** is easily assembled using an acrylic wreath on a silver-toned charger. For merry sparkle, insert **Snowflake Candle Pins** into a trio of pillar candles and place them in the center of the wreath. To serve zesty **Curried Chutney Spread**, only a **Beaded Spreader** will do. Provide plenty of apple wedges and celery sticks for nibbling.

Instructions and recipes for A Splendid Evening begin on page 128.

No holiday gathering is complete without an assortment of flavorful hors d'oeuvres. The festive delights include Boiled Shrimp with Zippy Cocktail Sauce *(clockwise from top)*, **Curried Chutney Spread**, Chicken Saté with Peanut Sauce, **Cheese Soufflé Sandwiches**, and Phyllo Sushi Rolls. Beneath this feast for the eyes and the taste buds lies a **Lavender Table Runner** adorned with bead circles and fringe.

Guests will raise glasses of Blushing Champagne Punch to toast the glory of your Beaded Cocktail Sets! Sparkling beads wrap around stemware in an instant, while silver snowflakes match the glass charms to their corresponding napkins. The wine glasses and matching Stained Glass Plates (*opposite, top*) get in the party spirit with easy-to-use stained glass paint.

Instructions and recipes for A Splendid Evening begin on page 128.

You'll be delighted at how quickly you can create **Easy Petits Fours** and **Chocolate-Raspberry Truffles**. And be sure to make extras, because these tempting treats won't last long! To serve, place on a silver tray embellished with glass stones — another fast-to-finish way to add glamour to this unforgettable night. Just adhere the stones with a glue that's recommended for glass or metal.

Updated *Classics*

Many contemporary homes feature a large, open living space adjacent to the kitchen, making it only natural to extend holiday décor into the cooking and dining areas. In this collection, we've combined classic red & white print fabrics with vintage Santas to create a look that's totally up-to-date!

An unexpected surprise: Instead of placing your Christmas tree in the sitting area, try setting it up near the kitchen or dining space! Reproductions of old metal ceiling tiles add interest to the **Tree Planter** that anchors our evergreen. For season-spanning accessories you can use all year, create a **Cinched Valance** or a **Covered Stool** in red and white.

Instructions for Updated Classics begin on page 135.

To make the family sofa a festive focal point for the living area, create a **Cross-Stitched Afghan** and add this beautiful St. Nicholas Pillow ... you can photocopy the same image we used, or use one of your favorites.

Embellished with fanciful wooden "appliqués" and bead garland, this Holiday Clock is far too pretty to put away after Christmas!

Instructions for Updated Classics *begin on page 135.*

Fabulous fun with fabric: Stitch a Festive Apron for the family cook and decorate a variety of Fabric-Lined Baskets to hold greeting cards, yummy treats, or an arrangement of greenery and ornaments. Make a trip to your local craft store to find topiaries, garlands, and other items to enhance your decorating theme — we chose bright red raspberries for a change of pace from the traditional cranberries.

If you don't have a fireplace mantel, improvise! We created a pretty **Painted Shelf** to display a **Berried Wreath** and **Framed Cross-Stitched Santa**, then added glass doorknobs to hang **Beaded Stockings** and other treasures.

A layer of micro beads forms the "frosted" finish on the photocopied **Santa** and **Clock Ornaments**. We gave them borders of silver-tone lead came (the edging strips used for stained glass) and shaped silver armature wire into spirals and curlicues for hangers. Berry garland and ribbon wraps around the boughs of the tree, while boxwood sprigs and red ball ornaments add fullness. A lighted **Treetop Wreath** (*shown on page 26*) completes the evergreen. For a little more light, cast a soft glow anywhere with a tasseled **Nightlight**.

Instructions for Updated Classics begin on page 135.

This Tiny Tag Tree is a delight to spy, as are the clay Reindeer standing under its branches. An assortment of Papier-Mâché Ornaments (*opposite*), adorned with nature-inspired cargo tags and gentle words, rests in a basin of buttons and greenery.

Instructions for A Season of Serenity begin on page 140.

A Season of *Serenity*

Above all, Christmas is a time to celebrate faith
and extend goodwill to others. These woodsy
creations use meaningful words and gifts from
nature to bestow a restful, reflective spirit
upon all who view them.

A naturally festive **Sisal Wreath** with glass ornaments shines in the window and welcomes your guests. A loop of wire-edged ribbon makes a quick and easy hanger, and we used hot glue to add a bay leaf garland, then filled in with extra leaves where needed. A simple bow tops the quick creation. Inside the house, a **Large Framed Collage** makes its textural appeal for a tranquil Christmas season. Who could possibly resist?

Why give packages that are only surprising on the inside? Your gifts gain originality when embellished with quick and easy artwork like textured torn paper or bay leaves trimmed into heart shapes. You can also fashion handmade tags with paper rosettes, a cluster of pearl beads, or your personally penned wishes for a joyous holiday season. Secure your tags with ribbons or raffia, then enjoy the delighted smiles these small yet meaningful efforts will yield.

Instructions for A Season of Serenity *begin on page 140.*

Dress the mantel with clay **Reindeer**, **Framed Words**, and white plates. Then add a forest of sisal trees, greenery, and beaded twigs. Use floral foam to stand small sisal trees in egg cups. And just for fun, incorporate your favorite Santa figurine.

Instructions for A Season of Serenity begin on page 140.

While it's pleasant to plan a serene holiday, it's also important to preserve joyous Christmas memories. Tuck mementos — such as snapshots, favorite recipes, greeting cards, and gift tags — into the envelopes of a Memory Album. You don't have to place them in any particular order or worry about tidiness just now. Wait until after the holidays to arrange your treasures on scrapbook pages. Then you'll have fun adding decorative touches while reminiscing at your leisure.

Instructions for A Season of Serenity *begin on page 140.*

Send out this year's greetings on very special keepsake cards — you can fashion them yourself using dried flowers and fruit, textured papers, buttons, raffia, and your own handwritten expressions of holiday joy. Follow our guidelines for **Creative Cards** on page 142, or experiment by combining your favorite natural elements with beads or old jewelry. You'll have as much fun creating these thoughtful cards as your recipients will receiving them.

Ranch Hand Roundup

Yippee ki-yi-ya! Round up your favorite ranch hands and rediscover the fun of a favorite childhood pastime with a cowboy-style Christmas party. We'll help you deck the halls and dress the table with colorful décor inspired by popular television shows and costumes from the 1950's.

Traditional red bandannas are plentiful and inexpensive at hobby and craft stores, and they're perfect for napkins! You can also use them to wrap up party favors — just tie up with twine and add a **Gift Tag** — or make a bright **Bandanna Garland** for the tree. Be sure to add a **Ten-Gallon Tree Topper!**

Instructions for Ranch Hand Roundup begin on page 144.

Herd 'em up and head 'em out! Painted Wooden Stars and candy-striped ribbon add cheer to Christmas Cowbells. (Check out the farmers' supply store to find an abundance of bells in various sizes.) Bed down the gifts on our fringed Painted Pony Tree Skirt, which is sewn using panels of painted muslin alternated with all-American denim.

No cowboy would ever be caught without his hat and boots — and neither should your tree! It's easy to gussy up nostalgic **Cowboy Hat Ornaments** with stars and holly. Western-style **Cowboy Boot Ornaments** are cut from faux suede and painted.

Round It Up!

To complete the tree, lasso the branches with a rope "lariat" and loops of ribbon; hang lots of shiny red balls for extra color. If you want to add fullness to the tree, simply tuck in sprigs of holly or other greenery.

Instructions for Ranch Hand Roundup begin on page 144.

Favorite Favors

For lasting reminders of your holiday roundup, use paint or fabric markers to personalize the cowboy hat or boot ornaments ... add the party date on the brim of the hat or the back of the boot.

When it's time to ring the dinner bell, make sure the table's dressed in cowpoke style! Colorful Horseshoe Candleholders add a festive glow, and you can fix up Decorated Drinking Glasses in a jiffy. The nifty Place Card Holders can double as photo holders (they're great for take-home favors!). Roll cutlery in a clean bandanna, then tie it up with twine and glue small Painted Wooden Stars to the ends.

Classic red ticking fabric makes a great backdrop for the **Star Table Topper**! We chose simple denim placemats and bright red and yellow dinnerware to finish the casual place settings. For the **Boot Centerpiece**, use your favorite greenery and berries (real or faux).

Instructions for Ranch Hand Roundup begin on page 144.

Cowbells jingle-jangle on the Rootin' Tootin' Wreath. We began with a grapevine wreath and added greenery, ribbon, stars, and a bandanna, too. (*Below*) Painted letters spell out a merry greeting on a collection of **Christmas Card Holders**.

(*Opposite*) **Horseshoe Stocking Holders** are natural companions for the fanciful **Cowboy Stockings** that march along the mantel. Paint a pair of cowboy boots with bright stars and holly ... use one as a holder for the **Candy Cane Bouquet**.

Instructions for Ranch Hand Roundup begin on page 144.

The Sharing

# of Christmas

Of course you want each gift you give to be as uniquely wonderful as the special people who'll receive them. With these original ideas for wrapping each treasure, and with so many excellent presents for you to create, you're sure to find the just-right combination for everyone on your Christmas list.

Wrap it up!

Wrap them, tie them, top them with a bow — there are as many ways to make your gifts beautiful as there are ways to make gifts. These very "present-able" finishing touches are quick to complete. And to really speed up your holiday gift-giving, organize your supplies. No more wrinkled wrapping paper, no more ragged ribbon … just lots of "oohs" and "aahs" when everyone sees what you've placed under the tree.

Just a little bit of creativity can make a collection of ordinary items into fun and useful things. For instance, a lidded box makes a perfect Ribbon Dispenser (*opposite*), keeping your spools tidy. Handmade rubber stamps quickly transform plain paper into festive **Stamped Gift Wrap**. And the hanging Wrap It Up Organizer puts all your gift-wrapping supplies in order while holding as many as ten rolls of wrapping paper.

Instructions for Wrap It Up! begin on page 148.

Joyous Wooden Gift Tags are more than just a way to identify your packages. After the gifts are opened, they also make nifty little ornaments for the Christmas tree. And here's a wonderful new use for scrapbooking materials: The Color-Blocked Shirt Box is covered with vellum and distinctively labeled with a trio of oval tags.

Instructions for Wrap It Up! begin on page 148.

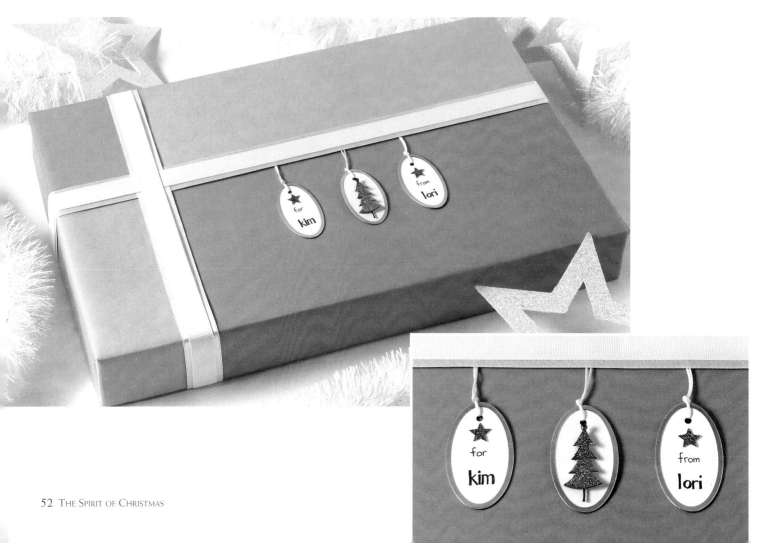

Your best gifts deserve a touch of elegance, and Festive Bows offer just that in three merry ways — each box is topped with a bow in the shape of a Christmas tree, an angel, or a poinsettia. And what better way to wrap a delicious loaf of homemade bread than to nestle it inside a chenille Placemat Wrap?

Maybe you know someone who could use a special place to store holiday photos? This **Christmas Photo Keeper** uses an empty cigar box and an old greeting card, and you can create it in just one evening! And for petite parcels with lots of personality, enclose little gifts in festive **Ribbon-Tied Boxes**.

Instructions for Wrap It Up! begin on page 148.

Luxury all the way through … once the boxes are opened, make your "giftees" feel extra-special with Terrific Trimmings. The inner wrappings of tissue paper are made lovely with novel embellishments. As every Santa knows, it's what you find on the inside that counts!

Tip:

Top ten must-have supplies for gift wrapping:

1. Metallic pens and markers
2. Self-adhesive labels and stickers
3. Faux greenery or berries
4. Ribbons (various widths and styles)
5. Assorted craft scissors
6. Cardstock in several colors
7. Hole punch
8. Two-sided adhesive tape
9. Gift wrap in solid colors
10. Colored tissue paper.

GIFTS
from HAND *to*
heart

Want to give the perfect gift? Invest a little of yourself in its creation! We've made each of these projects a snap to do, so you don't need any special skills to complete the best expression of your goodwill.

Anyone who loves beautiful things will treasure a set of **Glass Frame Pins**. And for each of your loved ones, make a quick and cozy **Biscuit Quilt**. It's a gift that will warm them twice — first with your affection, then with the softness of flannel!

Instructions for Gifts from Hand to Heart begin on page 154.

When you crochet using two strands of bulky yarn, you have time to make a **Fashion Scarf** for everyone on your gift list. Add feather-soft eyelash yarn to a few rows of stitches, and your toasty muffler takes on lots of touchable texture.

For a busy gal on the go, what better gift than a feminine **Watch Fob**? The timely trinket sparkles with beads and charms while hanging from a belt loop at the wearer's waist.

Instructions for Gifts from Hand to Heart begin on page 154.

A stylish **Marabou-Trimmed Purse** will make a sweet little girl feel like a sophisticated lady. And you'll be pleased with how easy it is to create the dainty handbag with poster board and fabric.

The **Story Time Tape Set** includes a classic Christmas tale and a recording of your voice as you read the book aloud, making it possible for you to be with your favorite youngster even when you're miles away.

Ultra-rich textures make this tote the most coveted gift you'll ever bestow. The **Bead-Fringed Bag** is fully lined and extra-sturdy, perfect for holding lots of necessities.

Capture a dazzling **Dragonfly Necklace** for her jewelry collection. Shimmering beads form the popular insect, making it a playful gift for ladies of any age.

Good things come in small (but pretty) packages. Our festive **Lotion Bars** require only three ingredients and are made using a microwave oven and inexpensive soap molds. While the bars harden, you can decorate the **Gift Boxes** with papers, stickers, or your choice of merry trims.

Recipients of the fabric-covered **Gift Box Ornaments** will know they've gotten two gifts in one! Each papier-mâché box is just the right size for holding jewelry or other small treasures, and will look lovely on the tree for many years to come.

Instructions for Gifts from Hand to Heart begin on page 154.

GREAT *goodies* TO *give*

It doesn't matter if you're a skilled chef or a fledgling cook — you'll have no trouble whipping up these incredible edibles to share with family & friends. Everyone will want to be on your gift list this year!

Creative packaging transforms a gift of food into a gift of good taste! You can decorate gift bags, tins, and boxes to hold snack mixes or confections, or try your hand at stitching up a fun felt Santa sack. Turn the page for more ideas!

Instructions for Great Goodies to Give *begin on page 159.*

Have a Merry Christmas
and Blessed New Year!

Christmas
WISHES

I will honor
Christmas
in my heart
and try to keep it
all the year.

To:
Jane

Sweets for thee...
A keepsake for the t

Merry
Christmas
The Clarks
2004

BASIC BEAN SOUP MIX

For a larger gift, layer 2 or 3 portions of beans. Be sure to give enough spice mix packets to prepare the beans.

Dried Bean Mix:
- 1 pound dried kidney beans
- 1 pound dried red lentils
- 1 pound green split peas
- 1 pound dried black beans
- 1 pound dried black-eyed peas

To prepare dried bean mix, combine beans in a large bowl. Divide the bean mixture into 5 equal portions (about 2$^1/_2$ cups each), and place in airtight containers.

Spice Mix:
- 5 teaspoons salt
- 5 teaspoons dried basil
- 5 teaspoons dried rosemary
- 5 teaspoons dried marjoram
- 2$^1/_2$ teaspoons black pepper
- 1$^1/_4$ teaspoons crushed red pepper
- 5 bay leaves

To prepare spice mix, combine first 6 ingredients in a bowl. Divide spice mix into 5 equal portions. Add a bay leaf to each portion. Place in small airtight containers. Give each spice mix with a dried bean mix and recipe for preparing soup.

Yield: 5 soup mixes

To Prepare Soup: Sort and wash 1 portion (about 2$^1/_2$ cups) dried bean mix, and place in a large Dutch oven. Cover with water to 2 inches above beans; cover and let stand 8 hours. Drain.

Combine the drained bean mixture, 6 to 8 cups water, and a smoked ham hock in a large Dutch oven; bring to a boil. Add 1 packet spice mix, 1 cup chopped onion, and 1 can (14.5 ounces) no-salt-added, diced tomatoes. Cover, reduce heat, and simmer 2 hours. Uncover; cook 1 hour. Discard bay leaf. Remove ham hock from soup. Remove meat from bone; shred meat with 2 forks. Return meat to soup. Serve warm.

Yield: 6 servings (1$^1/_2$ cups each)

You can't beat a bowl of hot, hearty soup on a blustery day! Pack our Basic Bean Soup Mix in a festive Soup Mix Jar for a warming meal.

This Salad Dressing Gift Set makes it easy to "dress" a salad in holiday style! We included jars of **Thick and Creamy Cheese Dressing** and **Balsamic Vinaigrette**.

Instructions for Great Goodies to Give begin on page 159.

THICK AND CREAMY CHEESE DRESSING

Use your favorite shredded or crumbled cheese or combination of cheeses for this delectable dressing. We used blue and Roquefort cheeses.

- 1 package (8 ounces) cream cheese, softened
- 1 container (8 ounces) sour cream
- 1 garlic clove, minced
- 1/4 cup half-and-half
- 1/4 teaspoon salt
- 3 tablespoons white wine vinegar
- 1 package (4 ounces) crumbled blue cheese
- 4 ounces Roquefort cheese, crumbled
- 2 tablespoons finely chopped parsley

Beat first 5 ingredients at medium speed with an electric mixer until blended. Gradually beat in vinegar. Stir in cheeses and parsley. Store in refrigerator.
Yield: 4 cups
Note: For a thinner consistency, add additional half-and-half.

BALSAMIC VINAIGRETTE

- 1/2 cup balsamic vinegar
- 3 tablespoons Dijon mustard
- 3 tablespoons honey
- 2 garlic cloves, minced
- 2 small shallots, minced
- 1/4 teaspoon salt
- 1/4 teaspoon pepper
- 1 cup olive oil

Whisk together first 7 ingredients until blended. Gradually whisk in olive oil. Store in refrigerator.
Yield: 1²/₃ cups

A cheese lover will appreciate a crock of **Buttery Blue Cheese Spread with Walnuts.** Include a bag of toast rounds and present it all in a handsome **Bay Leaf Wreath Box.**

Perfect for coffee-break time (*opposite*): **Chocolate-Hazelnut Coffee** is a quick, delicious treat, and it looks pretty in a **Painted Jar.** No one would ever guess that rich **Eggnog Tea Bread** began with a cake mix! The **Fabric-Covered Chest** can hold trinkets and treasures later.

Instructions for Great Goodies to Give begin on page 159.

BUTTERY BLUE CHEESE SPREAD WITH WALNUTS

This spread is also delicious served with apple and pear slices.

- 3 packages (8 ounces each) cream cheese, softened
- $^1/_2$ cup butter, softened
- 1 package (4 ounces) crumbled blue cheese
- $^1/_2$ cup diced walnuts, toasted
- $^1/_2$ cup chopped fresh chives
- $^1/_4$ cup cream sherry (optional)
  Garnishes: toasted diced walnuts, chopped fresh chives, and rosemary sprigs
- 2 French baguettes, sliced and toasted

Stir together first 5 ingredients and, if desired, sherry in a large bowl. Spoon into gift crocks; cover and chill mixture 8 hours. Let stand at room temperature to soften. Garnish, if desired, with walnuts, chives, and rosemary. Serve with toasted French baguette slices.
Yield: about 5 cups (24 appetizer servings)
Note: Spread can be frozen up to 1 month; thaw in refrigerator for 8 hours.

EGGNOG TEA BREAD

Use your extra holiday eggnog to make this sweet bread that makes enough little loaves for you and three friends.

- 1 package (16 ounces) pound cake mix
- $^3/_4$ cup refrigerated eggnog
- $^1/_2$ teaspoon ground nutmeg
- 2 large eggs
- 1 cup sifted powdered sugar
- 1 tablespoon refrigerated eggnog

Combine first 4 ingredients in a large mixing bowl; beat at medium speed with an electric mixer 3 minutes. Pour batter into 4 greased 6 x 3 x 2-inch loafpans. Bake at 350° for 30 minutes or until a wooden pick inserted in center comes out clean. Remove from pans; cool on wire racks.
Combine powdered sugar and 1 tablespoon eggnog, stirring well; spread over bread.
Yield: 4 loaves
Note: For a thinner icing, add additional eggnog.

CHOCOLATE-HAZELNUT COFFEE

These dry ingredients combine very quickly in a food processor.

- 1½ cups powdered nondairy coffee creamer
- 1 cup superfine sugar
- 1 cup hazelnut-flavored instant coffee granules
- ½ cup unsweetened cocoa

Combine ingredients in a medium bowl, stirring well. Store in an airtight container. Give with Serving Instructions.
Yield: about 3½ cups

Serving Instructions: Place 2½ tablespoons coffee mixture into a mug. Pour ¾ cup hot water into mug; stir until coffee mixture dissolves.

P rovide a quick supper for a busy family with hearty, ready-to-heat **Sicilian Spaghetti Sauce**. Round out your gift with a package of pasta and a bag of Parmesan nestled in a decorative **Hand-Painted Bowl**.

SICILIAN SPAGHETTI SAUCE

- 1 pound mild Italian sausage
- 1 pound lean ground beef
- 1 large onion, chopped
- 4 cloves garlic, minced
- 2 cans (29 ounces each) tomato sauce
- 2 cans (6 ounces each) Italian-style tomato paste
- 6 cups water
- 2 tablespoons sugar
- 2 teaspoons salt
- 1/4 cup minced fresh parsley
- 1/4 cup minced fresh basil
- 1/2 teaspoon ground red pepper
- 2 cups sliced fresh mushrooms
- 1/2 cup dry red wine
   Pasta
   Shredded Parmesan cheese

Remove casings from sausage, and discard. Cook sausage and ground beef in a Dutch oven over medium heat 6 minutes, stirring until meat crumbles. Add onion and garlic, and sauté 4 minutes or until beef and sausage are no longer pink. Drain and set aside. Wipe Dutch oven clean.

Combine tomato sauce and next 7 ingredients in Dutch oven; cook, stirring occasionally, 1 hour. Add sausage mixture, mushrooms, and wine. Cook, stirring occasionally, 1 hour and 30 minutes or until mixture thickens. Remove from heat and cool. Store in refrigerator. Give with pasta and cheese.

Instructions for Great Goodies to Give begin on page 159.

FRUIT CRUNCH SNACK MIX

1 package (10 ounces) red and green candy corn
1 package (10 ounces) pretzel nibblers
1 package (12 ounces) caramel popcorn and peanuts
2 packages (5.5 ounces each) banana chips
1 package (14 ounces) red and green candy-coated chocolate pieces
2 packages (6 ounces each) dried pineapple
2 packages (6 ounces each) sweetened dried cranberries
1 package (15 ounces) small pretzel twists
2 packages (7 ounces each) red and green small jelly beans

In a very large bowl, stir together all ingredients. Store in an airtight container.
Yield: about 38 cups

ITALIAN-SEASONED SNACK MIX

4 cups crispy corn-and-rice cereal
2 cups oyster crackers
2 cups small pretzel twists
$^1/_4$ cup butter, melted and cooled
2 egg whites, lightly beaten
$^1/_4$ cup grated Parmesan cheese
1 tablespoon dried Italian seasoning
Vegetable cooking spray

Combine first 3 ingredients in a large bowl. Combine butter and egg whites in a small bowl, stirring well with a wire whisk. Pour butter mixture over cereal mixture; toss lightly to coat. Sprinkle with cheese and Italian seasoning; toss lightly. Spread mixture in two 15 x 10 x 1-inch jellyroll pans coated with cooking spray. Bake at 300° for 25 minutes or until crisp, stirring occasionally. Cool completely. Store in an airtight container.
Yield: 10$^1/_2$ cups

Great gifts for a group: Sweet Fruit Crunch Snack Mix or savory Italian-Seasoned Snack Mix packaged in easy-to-trim Candy Cane Gift Sacks.

RICH REFRIGERATOR ROLLS

Variety is a bonus with these great-tasting rolls. Give several of each shape — cloverleaf, miniature, Parker House, and crescent!

- 1 cup water
- 1/2 cup butter or margarine
- 4 1/2 to 5 cups all-purpose flour
- 1/2 cup sugar
- 2 envelopes (1/4 ounce each) rapid-rise yeast
- 1 teaspoon salt
- 3 large eggs
- 1 large egg
- 1 tablespoon water
  Garnish: Sesame seeds, poppy seeds, chopped rosemary, or shredded Parmesan cheese

Combine water and butter in a saucepan; heat until butter melts, stirring occasionally. Cool to 120° to 130°.

Combine 2 cups flour, sugar, yeast, and salt in a large mixing bowl. Gradually add liquid mixture to flour mixture, beating at low speed with an electric mixer. Add 3 eggs, beating until well-blended. Beat 3 more minutes at medium speed. Gradually stir in enough remaining flour to make a soft dough.

Turn dough out onto a lightly floured surface, and knead 3 or 4 times. Place in a large well-greased bowl, turning to grease top. Cover and chill at least 8 hours.

Punch dough down, and divide dough into fourths. Shape each portion into Cloverleaf, Miniature, Parker House, or Crescent rolls. Lightly beat 1 egg and 1 tablespoon water. Brush rolls with egg mixture and garnish, as desired.

Cloverleaf Rolls: Using one-fourth of dough recipe, divide dough into 3 portions. Divide each portion into 6 pieces; shape each piece into a smooth ball. Place 3 balls in each cup of a greased muffin pan. Cover and let rise in a warm place (85°), free from drafts, 20 minutes or until doubled in bulk. Bake at 400° for 10 to 12 minutes or until golden.
Yield: 6 rolls

Miniature Rolls: Using one-fourth of dough recipe, divide dough into 3 portions. Divide each portion into 4 pieces; shape each piece into a smooth ball. Place 1 ball in each cup of a greased miniature muffin pan. Cover and let rise in a warm place (85°), free from drafts, 20 minutes or until doubled in bulk. Bake at 400° for 8 to 10 minutes or until golden.
Yield: 1 dozen rolls

Parker House Rolls: Using one-fourth of dough recipe, roll dough to 1/4-inch thickness on a lightly floured surface; cut with a 2-inch biscuit cutter. Brush tops lightly with melted butter. Using the dull edge of a knife, make an off-center crease in each round. Fold each round along crease, with larger portion on top. Place folded rolls in rows 2 inches apart on lightly greased baking sheets. Cover and let rise in a warm place (85°), free from drafts, 20 minutes or until doubled in bulk. Bake at 400° for 8 to 10 minutes or until golden.
Yield: 10 rolls

Crescent Rolls: Using one-fourth of dough recipe, roll dough into a 12-inch circle on a lightly floured surface; brush with melted butter. Cut into 10 wedges. Starting with wide end of wedge, roll toward point. Place rolls 2 to 3 inches apart on greased cookie sheets; curve to form a crescent shape. Cover and let rise in a warm place (85°), free from drafts, 20 minutes or until doubled in bulk. Bake at 400° for 8 to 10 minutes or until golden.
Yield: 10 rolls

Who can resist the aroma of fresh-baked yeast bread? This recipe for **Rich Refrigerator Rolls** lets you make four different types — cloverleaf, miniature, Parker House, and crescents — all from one basic dough. For added flavor and visual appeal, sprinkle with chopped herbs, shredded cheese, poppy seeds, or sesame seeds before baking. Pack them in a whimsical **Standing Santa Bag** for a home-baked treat.

Instructions for Great Goodies to Give begin on page 159.

A terrific trio: Caramel-Nut Popcorn Clusters, Hot Smoky Pecans, and Peppermint Pretzels will delight your favorite snackers! Use last year's Christmas cards to make the Decorated Tin.

CARAMEL-NUT POPCORN CLUSTERS

- 1 package (14 ounces) caramels
- 2 tablespoons whipping cream
- 12 cups popped popcorn
- 1 cup dry-roasted peanuts

Combine caramels and whipping cream in a glass bowl. Microwave at HIGH power 2 minutes or until melted, stirring mixture after each minute.

Place popcorn and peanuts in a large bowl. Drizzle with caramel sauce, tossing gently to coat. Place popcorn mixture on 2 lightly greased 15 x 10-inch jellyroll pans. Bake at 250° for 30 minutes, stirring after 15 minutes. Cool. Break into pieces; store in an airtight container.

Yield: about 13 cups

HOT SMOKY PECANS

- 3 tablespoons butter or margarine, melted
- 2 tablespoons soy sauce
- 2 teaspoons hot sauce
- 1 tablespoon Worcestershire sauce
- 4 cups pecan halves

Stir together first 4 ingredients; toss with pecans. Spread pecans in a single layer in a 15 x 10-inch jellyroll pan. Bake at 300°, stirring often, 25 minutes or until toasted. Cool. Store in an airtight container.

Yield: 4 cups

PEPPERMINT PRETZELS

Easy to make, hard to resist. This is one of those addictive salty-sweet snacks, and the addition of crushed peppermint makes it even better.

- 1 package (24 ounces) vanilla-flavored candy coating
- 1 package (15 ounces) pretzel twists
- 1 package (13 ounces) peppermint candies, crushed

Place candy coating in a large glass bowl, and microwave at HIGH power 1 1/2 minutes or until coating melts, stirring once. Dip pretzels into candy coating, covering completely; shake excess coating off of pretzels. Place coated pretzels on wax paper; sprinkle heavily with crushed peppermint. Let stand until candy coating is firm. Store pretzels in an airtight container.

Yield: about 15 dozen

CRANBERRY-CINNAMON GRANOLA BARS

- 4 cups low-fat granola cereal with raisins
- 1/2 cup firmly packed brown sugar
- 1/2 cup sweetened dried cranberries
- 1 teaspoon ground cinnamon
- 1 large egg
- 1 large egg white
- 2 teaspoons vanilla extract
  Vegetable cooking spray

Combine first 4 ingredients in a medium bowl. In a small bowl, combine egg, egg white, and vanilla; beat lightly until blended and stir into cereal mixture. Firmly press mixture evenly into a 9-inch square pan coated with cooking spray. Bake at 350° for 15 minutes or until golden. Cool in pan on a wire rack 5 minutes, and cut into bars. Store in an airtight container or wrap bars individually.

Yield: 8 bars

For yummy treats, package individually wrapped Cranberry-Cinnamon Granola Bars in foil gift wrap. You can add to the fun with a merry Granola Bar Wrapper and a Gift Tag Ornament.

Instructions for Great Goodies to Give begin on page 159.

The Tastes

# of Christmas

Warm and satisfying or sweet
and indulgent ... the tastes of
Christmas linger so favorably
in our memories. Enrich your
recollections of holiday
celebrations with these luscious
flavors and delicious scents.
It's time to treat yourself and
others to the best of the season,
and you can do it with ease!

ISING
on the
Cake

With tempting flavors like
rich chocolate orange,
robust fruit and nut, and
delicate almond, these
three heavenly cakes are
every bit as delicious
as they look.

Beneath the extravagantly thick layer of Grand
Marnier frosting, the Chocolate-Orange
Cream Cake stands tall with three layers of
cake and an orange-flavored filling. Encourage
guests to enjoy every decadent morsel,
for Christmas comes but once a year!

CHOCOLATE-ORANGE CREAM CAKE

Here's a fancy chocolate cake for sure, smothered in a swirly blanket of thick frosting.

- 1/2 cup Dutch process cocoa (such as Droste or Hershey's European-style)
- 1/2 cup boiling water
- 2/3 cup shortening
- 1 3/4 cups sugar
- 1 teaspoon orange extract
- 4 large eggs
- 1 1/2 teaspoons baking soda
- 1/4 teaspoon salt
- 2 1/2 cups all-purpose flour
- 1 1/2 cups buttermilk
  Cream Filling (recipe follows)
  Grand Marnier Frosting (recipe follows)
  Garnishes: orange slices and curls, chocolate curls

Combine cocoa and boiling water in a small bowl; stir until smooth. Cool completely.

Grease three 8" round cakepans; line with wax paper. Grease and flour wax paper and sides of pans. Set aside.

Beat shortening at medium speed of an electric mixer until creamy; gradually add sugar, beating until light and fluffy (about 5 minutes). Beat in chocolate mixture and orange extract. Add eggs, one at a time, beating after each addition. Combine soda, salt, and flour; add to shortening mixture alternately with buttermilk, beginning and ending with flour. Beat at low speed after each addition until blended. Pour batter into prepared pans. Bake at 350° for 25 minutes or until a wooden pick inserted in center comes out clean. Let cake layers cool in pans 10 minutes; remove from pans. Peel off wax paper, and let layers cool completely on wire racks.

Spread Cream Filling between layers to within 1/2" of edge. Spread Grand Marnier Frosting on sides and top of cake. Garnish, with orange and chocolate curls and orange slices.

Yield: one 3-layer cake

Note: For orange curl garnish, use a citrus peeler or knife to peel strips of rind from an orange; leaving white pith on fruit. Cut rind into long, thin strips. Wrap tightly around a pencil to create curls. Freeze briefly; then remove strips from pencil.

For chocolate curls, melt about 5 chocolate squares and pour into a jellyroll pan. Spread chocolate over pan. Chill about 10 minutes. Scrape across surface of chocolate with a long metal spatula, knife, teaspoon, or chocolate curler to form curls. The spatula and knife will form long, thin curls and the teaspoon and curler will form shorter curls. Return pan to refrigerator if chocolate becomes too soft. Use a toothpick to pick up curls.

CREAM FILLING

- 2 tablespoons all-purpose flour
- 1/3 cup milk
- 1/4 cup shortening
- 2 tablespoons butter or margarine, softened
- 1/2 teaspoon orange extract
- 1/8 teaspoon salt
- 2 cups sifted powdered sugar

Combine flour and milk in a small saucepan; cook over low heat, stirring constantly with a wire whisk, 3 minutes or until mixture resembles a soft frosting and is thick enough to hold its shape. (Do not boil.) Remove from heat; let cool.

Beat shortening and butter at medium speed of an electric mixer until creamy; add flour mixture, orange extract, and salt, beating well. Gradually add sugar, beating at high speed 4 to 5 minutes or until fluffy.

Yield: 1 1/2 cups filling

GRAND MARNIER FROSTING

- 1/2 cup butter, softened
- 3 (1-ounce) squares unsweetened chocolate, melted
- 1/4 cup Grand Marnier (orange liqueur) or orange juice
- 1/4 cup whipping cream
- 1 (16-ounce) package powdered sugar, sifted

Beat butter at medium speed of an electric mixer until creamy. Add chocolate, Grand Marnier, and whipping cream; beat well. Gradually add sugar, beating at high speed 5 minutes or until spreading consistency.

Yield: 3 cups frosting

BOURBON-LACED FRUIT AND NUT CAKE

Yes, this cake calls for a dozen eggs, but every rich bite is worth it!

- 1 cup butter or margarine, softened
- 2 cups sugar
- 3 1/2 cups sifted cake flour
- 3 1/2 teaspoons baking powder
- 3/4 teaspoon salt
- 1 cup milk
- 1 teaspoon vanilla extract
- 8 egg whites
  Fruit Filling (recipe follows)
  Frosting (recipe follows)

Grease four 9-inch round cakepans; line with wax paper. Grease wax paper, and set aside.

Beat butter at medium speed of an electric mixer until creamy; gradually add sugar, beating well. Combine flour, baking powder, and salt; add to butter mixture alternately with milk, beginning and ending with flour mixture. Mix at low speed after each addition until blended. Stir in vanilla.

Say "goodbye" to the hum-drum flavor and heavy texture of traditional fruitcake. Bourbon-Laced Fruit and Nut Cake embraces a rich custard-and-fruit filling between layers of fluffy cake, making every bite a pleasant new discovery.

Beat egg whites at high speed until stiff peaks form. Gently fold into flour mixture. Pour batter into prepared pans. Bake at 375° for 15 minutes or until a wooden pick inserted in center comes out clean. Cool in pans on wire racks 10 minutes; remove from pans, and let cool completely on wire racks.

Spread Fruit Filling between layers and on top of cake. Spread Frosting on sides of cake.

Yield: one 4-layer cake

FRUIT FILLING

- 1 1/2 cups raisins
- 1 1/2 cups red candied cherries, quartered
- 1 1/2 cups pecans, coarsely chopped
- 1 1/2 cups flaked coconut
- 12 egg yolks, lightly beaten
- 1 3/4 cups sugar
- 3/4 cup butter
- 1/2 teaspoon salt
- 1/2 cup bourbon

Place raisins in a small saucepan, and cover with water. Bring to a boil; cover, remove from heat, and let stand 5 minutes. Drain and pat dry. Combine raisins, cherries, chopped pecans, and coconut in a large bowl; set aside.

Combine egg yolks, sugar, butter, and salt in top of a double boiler; bring water to a boil. Reduce heat to medium; cook, stirring constantly, 20 minutes or until mixture is very thick. Add bourbon; stir well. Pour over fruit mixture, stirring well; let cool completely.

Yield: enough filling for one 4-layer cake

FROSTING

- 1 1/2 cups sugar
- 1/2 teaspoon cream of tartar
- 1/2 cup water
- 4 egg whites
- 1/2 teaspoon vanilla extract

Combine first 3 ingredients in a heavy saucepan. Cook over medium heat, stirring constantly, until mixture is clear. Cook, without stirring, until mixture reaches soft ball stage or until candy thermometer registers 240°. While syrup cooks, beat egg whites until soft peaks form; continue to beat, adding syrup in a heavy stream. Add vanilla; continue beating just until stiff peaks form and frosting is thick enough to spread. Spread frosting on cake.

Yield: 7 cups frosting

Surprise! Whether displayed as an edible centerpiece or given away as a thoughtful treat, the Gift Box Cake will delight the taste buds, as well as the eyes. It's the universal appeal of almond flavoring that makes this Christmas dessert more than just another pretty cake.

GIFT BOX CAKE

You can make your cake with 2 (18.25-ounce) packages white cake mix and 4 (16-ounce) containers ready-to-spread frosting.

- 1/2 cup butter or margarine, softened
- 1/2 cup shortening
- 2 cups sugar
- 2/3 cup water
- 2/3 cup milk
- 3 cups all-purpose flour
- 1 tablespoon baking powder
- 1 teaspoon salt
- 2 tablespoons vanilla extract
- 1 teaspoon almond extract
- 6 egg whites
  Powdered Sugar Frosting (recipe follows)
- 3 (4.5-ounce) packages chewy fruit rolls by the foot
- 1/3 cup clear and red sparkling sugar or edible glitter

Beat butter and shortening at medium speed with an electric mixer 1 minute or until creamy; gradually add sugar, beating well.

Combine water and milk. Combine flour, baking powder, and salt; add to sugar mixture alternately with milk mixture, beginning and ending with flour mixture. Stir in vanilla and almond extracts. Beat egg whites at high speed until stiff peaks form; fold into batter. Pour into 3 greased and floured 8-inch square baking pans. Bake at 350° for 18 minutes or until a wooden pick inserted in center comes out clean. Cool in pans on wire racks 10 minutes; remove from pans, and let cool completely on wire racks.

Reserve 2 cups Powdered Sugar Frosting. Spread 1/2 cup frosting into an 8-inch square on cake plate. Place bottom layer on icing square. Spread remaining frosting between layers and on top and sides of cake. Unroll fruit rolls (do not remove paper backing), and brush with water (photo 1). Sprinkle with sparkling sugar or edible glitter; let dry 15 minutes (photo 2).

Cut four (12-inch) pieces from fruit rolls. Remove paper backing, and arrange on top and sides of cake, pressing gently into frosting, to resemble ribbon. Spoon 1/2 cup reserved frosting onto center of cake, forming a 3-inch mound. Cut remaining fruit rolls into 4-inch pieces; remove paper backing. Fold each piece in half, resembling the loop of a bow; press cut ends into frosting mound, creating a large bow on top of cake (photo 3).

Spoon 1 1/2 cups reserved frosting into a decorating bag fitted with a large tip. Pipe a border around top and bottom edge of cake.

Yield: 1 (8-inch) cake

POWDERED SUGAR FROSTING

- 2 cups shortening
- 1 teaspoon salt
- 1 teaspoon almond extract
- 1 teaspoon vanilla extract
- 3 (16-ounce) packages powdered sugar, sifted
- 1 cup evaporated milk

Beat first 4 ingredients at medium speed with a heavy-duty electric mixer until blended. Add powdered sugar alternately with milk, beating at low speed until blended after each addition. Beat at medium speed 8 minutes or until light and fluffy.

Yield: 7 cups frosting

Note: Frosting may be stored in refrigerator up to 2 weeks. If using a portable mixer, prepare frosting in 2 batches.

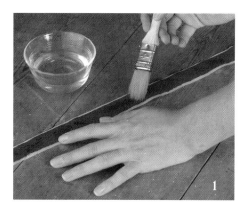

hearty, healthy
HOLIDAY FARE

If you want all the enjoyment of a rich holiday feast, but don't want to trade your favorite Christmas sweater for something in a larger size, then this deliciously hearty meal is for you! And no one will be able to tell that calories have been cut from any of these flavor-packed dishes.

Succulent pork and a sweet, tangy sauce will make you forget that this substantial entrée is lean on calories. Pork Tenderloin with Gingered Cranberries is also an elegant, easy-to-serve choice for your main dish.

Southern Corn Bread Dressing

1 can (12 ounces) refrigerated buttermilk biscuits
  Speckled Corn Bread, crumbled (recipe follows)
2 tablespoons rubbed sage
1 teaspoon poultry seasoning
1/4 to 1/2 teaspoon pepper
1 teaspoon margarine
  Cooking spray
1 cup chopped celery
1 cup chopped onion
4 cans (10 1/2 ounces each) low-salt chicken broth
2 large egg whites, lightly beaten

Bake biscuits according to package directions; let cool. Tear 8 of the biscuits into small pieces; reserve remaining 2 for another use. Combine crumbled corn bread, torn biscuits, sage, poultry seasoning, and pepper in a large bowl; set aside. Preheat oven to 350°. Melt margarine in a medium nonstick skillet coated with cooking spray. Sauté celery and onion until tender. Let cool slightly. Add vegetable mixture to dressing mixture, and gently stir in broth and egg whites. Spoon mixture into a 13 x 9-inch baking dish coated with cooking spray. Bake at 350° for 55 minutes.

Yield: 10 servings
Per Serving: Calories 262 (25% from fat); Fat 7.2g (sat 1.6g, mono 3.2g, poly 1.3g); Protein 8.8g; Carbohydrate 9.3g; Fiber 1.3g; Cholesterol 1mg; Iron 3.2mg; Sodium 782mg; Calcium 150mg

Speckled Corn Bread

1 teaspoon margarine
  Cooking spray
1 cup frozen whole-kernel corn, thawed
1 cup chopped red bell pepper
1 1/3 cups self-rising yellow cornmeal mix
2/3 cup self-rising flour
1 teaspoon sugar
1/8 teaspoon ground red pepper
1 1/4 cups skim milk
2 large egg whites, lightly beaten

Preheat oven to 400°. Melt margarine in a nonstick skillet coated with cooking spray. Sauté corn and bell pepper 8 minutes or until corn is lightly browned and pepper is tender; stir frequently. Let cool. Combine vegetable mixture, cornmeal mix, flour, sugar, and ground red pepper in a large bowl; add milk and egg whites, stirring until moist. Pour batter into a 9-inch round cake pan coated with cooking spray. Bake at 400° for 30 minutes or until a wooden pick inserted in center comes out clean. Remove from pan; let cool on a wire rack.

Yield: 12 servings (serving size: 1 wedge)
Per Serving: Calories 100 (9% from fat); Fat 1g (sat 0.2g, mono 0.3g, poly 0.4g); Protein 3.8g; Carbohydrate 19.8g; Fiber 0.5g; Cholesterol 1mg; Iron 1.3mg; Sodium 381mg; Calcium 105mg

Pork Tenderloin with Gingered Cranberries

Dried cranberries, sweetened and unsweetened, are now readily available in most supermarkets. We preferred the sweetened cranberries for this recipe.

1 pork tenderloin (about 1 pound), trimmed
  Cooking spray
2 teaspoons Worcestershire sauce
1/2 teaspoon cracked black pepper
1/4 teaspoon salt
1/2 cup dry red wine
1/2 cup orange juice
1/2 cup dried cranberries
1/8 teaspoon ground cinnamon
1/2 teaspoon minced, peeled fresh ginger

Preheat oven to 425°. Place pork in a 13 x 9-inch baking pan coated with cooking spray. Drizzle with Worcestershire sauce; sprinkle with pepper and salt. Bake at 425° for 25 to 30 minutes or until a meat thermometer inserted into thickest portion of pork registers 160°. Let stand 5 minutes. Combine red wine and next 3 ingredients in a small saucepan; bring to a boil. Boil, uncovered, 5 minutes, stirring frequently. Remove from heat; stir in ginger. Spoon sauce over pork.

Yield: 4 servings (serving size: 3 ounces pork and about 2 tablespoons sauce)
Per Serving: Calories 220 (17% from fat); Protein 24.1g; Fat 4.0g (sat 1.4g); Carbohydrate 15.2g; Fiber 1.3g; Cholesterol 74mg; Iron 1.8mg; Sodium 233mg; Calcium 17mg

Butternut Squash with Maple Syrup

1 butternut squash (about 2 pounds), peeled and cubed
2 1/2 tablespoons pure maple syrup
1 tablespoon butter, softened
1/4 teaspoon salt
1/8 teaspoon pepper

Steam squash, covered, 25 minutes or until very tender. Combine squash, syrup, and remaining ingredients in a large bowl; mash squash mixture with a potato masher.

Yield: 4 servings (serving size: 1/2 cup)
Per Serving: Calories 111 (24% from fat); Protein 2.1g; Fat 3.2g (sat 1.9g); Carbohydrate 20.9g; Fiber 2.1g; Cholesterol 8mg; Iron 1.0mg; Sodium 183mg; Calcium 54mg

Calorie Reducers

Instead of Using:	Use:
One whole egg	Two egg whites
Cream cheese	Fat-free cream cheese or Neufchâtel cheese
Whipping cream	Evaporated fat-free milk, chilled and whipped
Fudge sauce	Chocolate syrup

Side dishes like low-cal Carrot Soufflé and Green Beans with Lemon and Browned Garlic impart all the flavor you expect of a holiday meal, and will keep the plates coming back for more.

CARROT SOUFFLÉ

Because this dish contains no beaten egg whites, it is not a true soufflé — the name is derived from its light airy texture. Similar in color and flavor to sweet potato casserole, it pairs well with ham or turkey.

    7   cups chopped carrot
    2/3 cup granulated sugar
    1/4 cup fat-free sour cream
    3   tablespoons all-purpose flour
    2   tablespoons butter, melted
    1   teaspoon baking powder
    1   teaspoon vanilla extract
    1/4 teaspoon salt
    3   large eggs, lightly beaten
         Cooking spray
    1   teaspoon powdered sugar

Preheat oven to 350°. Cook carrot in boiling water 15 minutes or until very tender; drain. Place carrot in a food processor; process until smooth. Add granulated sugar and next 7 ingredients; pulse to combine. Pour mixture into a 2-quart baking dish coated with cooking spray. Bake at 350° for 50 minutes or until puffed and set. Sprinkle with powdered sugar.
Yield: 8 servings (serving size: 1/2 cup)
Per Serving: Calories 187 (25% from fat); Fat 5.1g (sat 2.5g, mono 1.6g, poly 0.5g); Protein 4.2g; Carbohydrate 32.3g; Fiber 3.5g; Cholesterol 88mg; Iron 1.1mg; Sodium 233mg; Calcium 86mg

GREEN BEANS WITH LEMON AND BROWNED GARLIC

    3/4   cup water
    1   pound green beans, trimmed
    2 1/2 teaspoons olive oil
    3   garlic cloves, minced
    3   tablespoons fresh lemon juice
    1/8   teaspoon salt
    1/8   teaspoon pepper

Bring water to a boil in a large nonstick skillet; add beans. Cook 3 minutes; drain and set aside. Heat oil in skillet over medium-high heat. Add garlic and beans, and sauté 1 minute. Add juice, salt, and pepper; sauté 1 minute.
Yield: 4 servings (serving size: 1 cup)
Per Serving: Calories 66 (40% from fat); Fat 2.9g (sat 0.4g, mono 2g, poly 0.3g); Protein 2.3g; Carbohydrate 9.9g; Fiber 2.4g; Cholesterol 0mg; Iron 1.2mg; Sodium 78mg; Calcium 47mg

CHOCOLATE CHUNK BREAD PUDDINGS

Try not to chop the chocolate too finely so you'll have good-sized chunks to bite into. Hawaiian bread is a soft, sweet bread found in the bakery section of most grocery stores. Leftovers are good for ham and Swiss sandwiches.

    1³/₄ cups (¹/₂-inch) cubed Hawaiian sweet bread
     ²/₃ cup 2% reduced-fat milk
       2 tablespoons sugar
    1¹/₂ tablespoons unsweetened cocoa
       1 tablespoon Kahlúa (coffee-flavored liqueur)
     ¹/₂ teaspoon vanilla extract
       1 large egg, lightly beaten
          Cooking spray
       1 ounce semisweet chocolate, coarsely chopped
       2 tablespoons frozen fat-free whipped topping, thawed

Preheat oven to 350°. Arrange bread cubes in a single layer on a baking sheet. Bake at 350° for 5 minutes or until toasted. Remove bread from oven; decrease oven temperature to 325°. Combine milk and next 5 ingredients in a medium bowl, stirring well with a whisk. Add bread, tossing gently to coat. Cover and chill 30 minutes or up to 4 hours.

Divide half of bread mixture evenly between 2 (6-ounce) ramekins or custard cups coated with cooking spray; sprinkle evenly with half of chocolate. Divide remaining bread mixture between ramekins; top with remaining chocolate. Place ramekins in an 8-inch square baking pan; add hot water to pan to a depth of 1 inch. Bake at 325° for 35 minutes or until set. Serve each pudding warm with 1 tablespoon whipped topping.

Yield: 2 servings
Per Serving: Calories 319 (30% from fat); Fat 10.6g (sat 5.2g, mono 3.6g, poly 0.8g); Protein 9.8g; Carbohydrate 45.3g; Fiber 2.1g; Cholesterol 121mg; Iron 1.8mg; Sodium 141mg; Calcium 125mg

CLASSIC PECAN PIE

To pack lots of pecans in the filling, we kept the fat in this easy piecrust to a minimum, resulting in a biscuitlike crust.

Crust
       1 cup all-purpose flour
       2 tablespoons granulated sugar
     ¹/₂ teaspoon baking powder
     ¹/₄ teaspoon salt
     ¹/₄ cup fat-free milk
       1 tablespoon butter or stick margarine, melted
          Cooking spray
Filling
       1 large egg
       4 large egg whites
       1 cup light or dark-colored corn syrup
     ²/₃ cup packed dark brown sugar
     ¹/₄ teaspoon salt
       1 cup pecan halves
       1 teaspoon vanilla extract

To prepare crust, lightly spoon flour into a dry measuring cup; level with a knife. Combine flour, granulated sugar, baking powder, and ¹/₄ teaspoon salt in a bowl. Add milk and butter; toss with a fork until moist. Press mixture gently into a 4-inch circle on heavy-duty plastic wrap; cover with additional plastic wrap. Roll dough, still covered, to an 11-inch circle. Freeze 10 minutes or until plastic wrap can be easily removed. Remove 1 sheet of plastic wrap; fit dough into a 9-inch pie plate coated with cooking spray. Remove top sheet of plastic wrap. Fold edges under; flute. Preheat oven to 350°. To prepare the filling, beat the egg and the next 4 ingredients at medium speed of a mixer until well-blended. Stir in the pecan halves and the vanilla extract. Pour the mixture into the prepared crust. Bake the pie at 350° for 20 minutes, then cover with foil. Bake the pie an additional 20 minutes or until a knife inserted 1 inch from the edge comes out clean. Do not overbake. Cool pie on a wire rack.

Yield: 10 servings (serving size: 1 wedge)
Per Serving: Calories 288 (29% from fat); Fat 9.2g (sat 1.5g, mono 5.1g, poly 2g); Protein 4.3g; Carbohydrate 48.1g; Fiber 1g; Cholesterol 25mg; Iron 1.1mg; Sodium 253mg; Calcium 52mg

Dessert? Yes, please! Chocolate Chunk Bread Puddings and Classic Pecan Pie are amazingly good, delightfully rich, and oh-so-easy on the waistline. They're superb finales to your hearty, healthy, holiday meal.

CLASSIC CHRISTMAS *sweets*

It just wouldn't be Christmas without plenty of tempting treats from the kitchen. As the Yuletide celebrations begin, offer these tried-and-true delights. They'll evoke fond reminiscences of holidays past while creating new memories to cherish for years to come.

Bite-size Christmas Tassies offer the fruity tang of cranberries in a mellow cream cheese crust. Melt-In-Your-Mouth Iced Sugar Cookies will remind you of visits to Grandma's house. And you'll go nuts over the simplicity of Super Chocolate Candy.

CHRISTMAS TASSIES

Serve these bite-size cranberry-nut gems when family and friends drop in during the holidays.

- 1/2 cup butter or margarine, softened
- 1 (3-ounce) package cream cheese, softened
- 1 cup all-purpose flour
  Vegetable cooking spray
- 1 large egg, beaten
- 3/4 cup firmly packed brown sugar
- 1 tablespoon butter or margarine, melted
- 1 teaspoon grated orange rind
- 1/2 cup chopped fresh cranberries
- 1/2 cup chopped pecans

Beat 1/2 cup butter and cream cheese at medium speed of an electric mixer until creamy. Gradually add flour, beating well. Cover and chill 1 hour.

Shape dough into 24 (1-inch) balls; press balls into miniature (1 3/4-inch) muffin pans lightly coated with cooking spray. Set aside. Combine egg and next 3 ingredients; stir in cranberries and pecans. Spoon 1 tablespoon mixture into each shell. Bake at 325° for 30 to 33 minutes or until filling is set. Remove from pans immediately, and let cool completely on wire racks.

Yield: 2 dozen tassies

MELT-IN-YOUR-MOUTH ICED SUGAR COOKIES

- 1 cup butter, softened
- 1 1/2 cups sugar
- 1 large egg
- 3 cups all-purpose flour
- 1/2 teaspoon baking soda
- 1/2 teaspoon salt
- 1 teaspoon cream of tartar
- 2 teaspoons vanilla extract
  Royal Icing (recipe follows)
  Assorted colors paste food coloring
  Assorted candies
  Decorator sprinkles

Beat butter at medium speed of an electric mixer 2 minutes or until creamy. Gradually add sugar, beating well. Add egg; beat well. Combine flour, baking soda, salt, and cream of tartar. Add to butter mixture, beating at low speed just until blended. Stir in vanilla. Roll dough to 1/4" thickness on a lightly floured surface. Cut with decorative 3" cookie cutters. Place 1" apart on ungreased cookie sheets. Bake at 350° for 9 minutes. Cool completely on wire racks.

Spoon about 2/3 cup white Royal Icing into a decorating bag fitted with decorating tip #3 (small round tip). Pipe white icing to outline cookies and to outline detail desired inside cookies. Divide remaining Royal Icing into a separate bowl for each color desired; color as desired with paste food coloring. Slowly stir just enough water into each bowl of icing to make "flow-in icing" that is still thick but flows into a smooth surface after stirring. (Add water a little at a time; if flow-in icing is too watery, it may not dry properly and may run under outline into another color area.) Fill decorating bags (using no tips) about half full of flow-in icing. Snip off small tip of cone. Pipe desired colors of icing to cover areas between the Royal Icing outlines; spread icing into corners and hard-to-reach areas using a wooden pick, as necessary. Add flow-in icing 1 color at a time, allowing icing to dry before changing colors. Avoid using excess icing, or it will spill over into another color area. If air bubbles form in icing, use a sterilized straight pin to remove them. Decorate with assorted candies and decorator sprinkles while icing is still wet.

Yield: 3 1/2 dozen cookies

ROYAL ICING

This icing dries very quickly, so keep it covered at all times with a damp cloth to help keep it moist.

- 3 large eggs
- 1 (16-ounce) package powdered sugar, divided
- 1/2 teaspoon cream of tartar

Combine egg whites, 1 cup powdered sugar, and cream of tartar in top of a double boiler. Place over simmering water. Cook, stirring constantly with a wire whisk, 9 minutes or until mixture reaches 160°. Remove from heat. Transfer to a large mixing bowl, and add remaining powdered sugar. Beat at high speed of an electric mixer 5 to 8 minutes or until stiff peaks form.

Yield: 2 cups icing

SUPER CHOCOLATE CANDY

- 12 ounces peanut butter morsels
- 1 package (4 ounces) sweet baking chocolate
- 1 1/2 cups pecan halves
- 1/2 cup flaked coconut (optional)

Cook peanut butter morsels and chocolate in a medium-size heavy saucepan over low heat until melted, stirring occasionally. Stir in pecans and coconut, if desired. Drop by rounded teaspoonfuls onto wax paper, and let cool completely.

Yield: about 24 pieces candy

They look as though you spent an entire day creating them, but Chocolate-Caramel Thumbprints are easily made with simple ingredients. You'll have fun topping the tasty treasures with a drizzle of rich, melted chocolate.

CHOCOLATE-CARAMEL THUMBPRINTS

- 3/4 cup butter or margarine, softened
- 1/2 cup sugar
- 2 (1-ounce) squares semisweet chocolate, melted
- 1 egg yolk
- 2 teaspoons vanilla extract
- 1 1/2 cups all-purpose flour
- 1/4 teaspoon baking soda
- 1/2 teaspoon salt
- 3/4 cup very finely chopped pecans
- 16 milk caramels
- 2 1/2 tablespoons whipping cream
- 2/3 cup semisweet chocolate morsels
- 2 teaspoons shortening

Beat butter at medium speed of an electric mixer until creamy; gradually add sugar, beating well. Add melted chocolate and egg yolk, beating until blended. Stir in vanilla. Combine flour, soda, and salt; add to butter mixture, beating well.

Shape dough into 1" balls; roll balls in chopped pecans. Place balls 1" apart on greased cookie sheets. Press thumb gently into center of each ball, leaving an indentation. Bake at 350° for 12 minutes or until set.

Meanwhile, combine caramels and whipping cream in top of a double boiler over simmering water. Cook over medium-low heat, stirring constantly, until caramels melt and mixture is smooth. Remove cookies from oven; cool slightly, and press center of each cookie again. Quickly spoon 3/4 teaspoon caramel mixture into center of each cookie. Remove cookies to wire racks to cool.

Place chocolate morsels and shortening in a 1-quart zip-top freezer bag; seal bag. Microwave at HIGH 1 to 1 1/2 minutes; squeeze bag until chocolate melts. Snip a tiny hole in one corner of bag, using scissors. Drizzle chocolate over cooled cookies.

Yield: about 2 1/2 dozen cookies

The crisp texture of Coffee-Hazelnut Biscotti will make the Italian-style pastry into a new Christmas snacking tradition at your house. Serve the mildly sweet biscotti with hot coffee for dunking. And for simple-to-create treats that pack a lot of flavor, bake a batch of Butter Meltaways with Lemon Frosting.

COFFEE-HAZELNUT BISCOTTI

    2 tablespoons Frangelico (hazelnut-flavored liqueur)
    2 tablespoons unsweetened cocoa
    1 teaspoon instant espresso or 2 teaspoons instant
         coffee granules
    1 teaspoon vegetable oil
    2 large egg whites
    1 large egg
 1 1/3 cups all-purpose flour
  1/2 cup whole-wheat flour
  1/2 cup granulated sugar
  1/2 cup packed brown sugar
  1/2 cup coarsely chopped toasted hazelnuts, divided
    1 teaspoon baking soda
  1/8 teaspoon salt
    2 teaspoons ground coffee beans
       Cooking spray

Preheat oven to 300°. Place liqueur in a small bowl. Microwave at high 10 seconds. Stir in cocoa and espresso until smooth. Add oil, egg whites, and egg, stirring with a whisk until blended.

Lightly spoon flours into dry measuring cups; level with a knife. Place flours, sugars, 2 tablespoons hazelnuts, baking soda, and salt in a food processor; process until hazelnuts are ground. Add ground coffee; pulse 2 times or until blended. With processor on, slowly add liqueur mixture through food chute; process until dough forms a ball. Add 6 tablespoons hazelnuts; pulse 5 times or until blended (dough will be sticky). Turn dough out onto a floured surface; knead lightly 4 to 5 times. Divide dough into 3 equal portions, shaping each portion into a 10-inch-long roll. Place rolls 3 inches apart on a large baking sheet coated with cooking spray. Bake at 300° for 28 minutes.

Remove rolls from baking sheet; cool 10 minutes on a wire rack. Cut each roll diagonally into 20 (1/2-inch) slices. Place slices, cut sides down, on baking sheets. Bake at 300° for 20 minutes. Turn cookies over; bake an additional 10 minutes (cookies will be slightly soft in center but will harden as they cool). Remove from baking sheets; cool completely on wire racks.

Yield: 5 dozen biscotti (serving size: 1 biscotto)
Note: To toast hazelnuts, place on a baking sheet and bake at 350° for 15 minutes, stirring once. Turn nuts out onto a towel. Roll up towel and rub off skins. Chop nuts.

Butter Meltaways with Lemon Frosting

We recommend using only butter for this recipe — it makes these tea cookies wonderfully short.

- 1 cup butter, softened
- 1/3 cup sifted powdered sugar
- 1 1/4 cups all-purpose flour
- 3/4 cup cornstarch
  Lemon Frosting (recipe follows)

Beat butter at medium speed of an electric mixer until creamy; gradually add powdered sugar, beating well. Combine flour and cornstarch; gradually add to butter mixture, beating well. Shape dough into 2 (6-inch) logs, and wrap in wax paper dusted with powdered sugar. Chill at least 6 hours.

Unwrap dough; cut each log into 18 slices, and place slices 2 inches apart on greased cookie sheets. Bake at 350° for 12 minutes. Remove cookies to a wire rack, and let cool completely. Spread cookies with Lemon Frosting.

Yield: 3 dozen cookies

Lemon Frosting

- 1/4 cup butter, softened
- 1 1/2 cups sifted powdered sugar
- 1 tablespoon fresh lemon juice
- 1 tablespoon grated lemon rind

Beat butter at medium speed of an electric mixer until creamy; gradually add powdered sugar, beating until blended. Add lemon juice, beating until spreading consistency; stir in lemon rind.

Yield: 3/4 cup frosting

Chewy Brownie Grahams

You won't believe these fudgy-chewy brownies have only five ingredients and still received the highest test kitchen rating. The thick batter is loaded with chocolate graham cracker crumbs.

- 1 cup (6 ounces) semisweet chocolate morsels
- 1/2 cup creamy or chunky peanut butter
- 1 (14-ounce) can sweetened condensed milk
- 1/2 cup coarsely chopped pecans, toasted
- 2 cups chocolate graham cracker crumbs or chocolate wafer cookie crumbs

Combine first 3 ingredients in a saucepan; cook over medium heat, stirring constantly, until morsels and peanut butter melt. Remove from heat. Stir in pecans and chocolate crumbs. (Batter will be very thick.) Press batter into a heavily greased 8" square pan. Bake at 350° for 24 minutes. Let cool in pan. Cut into 2" squares.

Yield: 16 brownies

White Chocolate-Macadamia Fudge

- 3 cups (18 ounces) white chocolate morsels
- 1 1/2 cups miniature marshmallows
- 1 (14-ounce) can sweetened condensed milk
- 2 teaspoons grated orange rind
- 1 teaspoon vanilla extract
- 1/8 teaspoon salt
- 1 cup chopped macadamia nuts, toasted

Line a 9" square pan with aluminum foil; lightly grease foil. Cook first 3 ingredients in a heavy saucepan over medium heat, stirring constantly, 10 to 11 minutes or until smooth. Remove from heat, and stir in orange rind, vanilla, and salt until blended. Stir in nuts. Pour fudge into prepared pan. Cover and chill at least 4 hours or until firm. Cut fudge into squares, and store in refrigerator.

Yield: 2 pounds fudge

Fudge is as much a part of the holidays as Christmas carols and colorful trees, but the zesty goodness of orange rind and the crunch of toasted macadamia nuts makes a delicious difference in White Chocolate-Macadamia Fudge.

LITTLE CHOCOLATE-KAHLÚA FRUITCAKES

If you think you don't like fruitcake, give these a try. They're gooey and brownielike and unforgettable!

- 1 cup butter
- 6 (1-ounce) squares semisweet chocolate
- 1 teaspoon instant coffee granules
- 1 cup firmly packed brown sugar
- 3 large eggs, separated
- 1/4 cup plus 2 tablespoons Kahlúa or other coffee-flavored liqueur, divided
- 1 teaspoon vanilla extract
- 2 cups all-purpose flour, divided
- 1/2 teaspoon baking soda
- 1/4 teaspoon salt
- 1 (10-ounce) container whole pitted dates, chopped (about 1 3/4 cups)
- 1 1/2 cups chopped pecans, toasted
- 1 cup semisweet chocolate mega-morsels or regular morsels
- 3/4 cup dried apricots, chopped
  Additional Kahlúa

Grease five 6" x 3" x 2" loafpans. Line bottoms of loafpans with wax paper; set aside. Melt butter and chocolate in a heavy saucepan over low heat, stirring often. Stir in coffee granules. Remove mixture from heat, and let cool 15 minutes. Pour into a large bowl. Stir in brown sugar. Add egg yolks, stirring well. Add 2 tablespoons Kahlúa and vanilla; stir well. Combine 1 1/2 cups flour, soda, and salt; add to chocolate mixture. Combine dates and next 3 ingredients; sprinkle with remaining 1/2 cup flour, tossing to coat. Stir fruit mixture into batter. Beat egg whites at high speed of an electric mixer until stiff peaks form; fold into batter. Spoon batter evenly into prepared pans. Bake at 300° for 1 hour and 15 minutes or until a wooden pick inserted in center comes out clean. Let cool in pans on a wire rack 10 minutes; remove from pans, and brush loaves with remaining 1/4 cup Kahlúa. Let cool completely on a wire rack.

Wrap fruitcakes in Kahlúa-soaked cheesecloth. Store in an airtight container in a cool place at least 1 week before serving. Pour a small amount of Kahlúa over each loaf every week up to 1 month. To serve, slice with an electric knife.
Yield: 5 loaves

MOLASSES CRINKLES

- 1/4 cup margarine, softened
- 3/4 cup plus 1 1/2 tablespoons sugar, divided
- 1/4 cup molasses
- 1 egg
- 2 cups all-purpose flour
- 2 teaspoons baking soda
- 1/4 teaspoon salt
- 1 3/4 teaspoons ground cinnamon, divided
  Vegetable cooking spray

Beat margarine at medium speed of an electric mixer until creamy; gradually add 3/4 cup sugar, beating well. Add molasses and egg; beat well. Combine flour, baking soda, salt, and 1 1/2 teaspoons ground cinnamon in a small bowl, stirring well. Gradually add flour mixture to margarine mixture, beating until blended. Cover dough, and chill 1 hour.

Combine remaining 1 1/2 tablespoons sugar and 1/4 teaspoon ground cinnamon in a small bowl, and set aside. Shape dough into 48 (1-inch) balls; roll balls in sugar mixture. Place balls, 2 inches apart, on cookie sheets coated with cooking spray. Bake at 350° for 8 minutes or until golden. Cool slightly on cookie sheets. Remove from cookie sheets, and cool completely on wire racks.
Yield: 4 dozen cookies

DIVINITY

- 3 egg whites
- 2 1/2 cups sugar
- 1/2 cup light corn syrup
- 1/2 cup water
- 1/4 teaspoon salt
- 1 teaspoon vanilla extract
- 1 cup chopped pecans, toasted

Beat egg whites at high speed with an electric mixer until soft peaks form. Combine sugar, corn syrup, water, and salt in a heavy 2-quart saucepan. Bring to a boil, stirring constantly. Wash down sugar crystals with a brush dipped in hot water. Boil until mixture reaches hard ball stage, 260° on a candy thermometer (about 10 minutes). With mixer running at high speed, pour syrup over egg whites in a pencil-size stream; beat in vanilla. Beat until mixture thickens and mounds slightly when dropped from a spoon (about 10 minutes in a glass bowl, less in a metal one). Stir in pecans. Quickly drop candy onto wax paper by rounded teaspoonfuls. Cool completely.
Yield: 3 dozen candies (1 1/2 pounds)

Of course we had to include the most beloved cookies of Christmas — molasses-sweetened Gingerbread Men have currant faces and wear cinnamon candy for buttons. The old-fashioned goodness of Divinity completes this timeless collection of classic treats.

GINGERBREAD MEN

A few decorations are simple enough for little helping hands. Reroll the dough to use every scrap.

1	cup shortening
1	cup sugar
1	cup molasses
2	tablespoons white vinegar
1	large egg
5	cups all-purpose flour
1 1/2	teaspoons baking soda
1/2	teaspoon salt
3	teaspoons ground ginger
1	teaspoon ground cloves
1	teaspoon ground cinnamon
	Currants
	Red cinnamon candies

Beat shortening at medium speed of an electric mixer until creamy; gradually add sugar, beating well. Add molasses, vinegar, and egg; beat well. Combine flour and next 5 ingredients; gradually add to shortening mixture, beating well. Shape dough into a ball; wrap in plastic wrap, and chill 8 hours.

Divide dough in half. Work with 1 portion of dough at a time, storing remainder in refrigerator. Roll each portion of dough to 1/8" thickness on a well-floured surface. Cut with a 4" gingerbread man cookie cutter; place on ungreased cookie sheets, using a floured spatula to lift cookies from work surface. Press currants into dough to form eyes and mouth. Press 4 cinnamon candies into dough for nose and buttons. Bake at 375° for 7 to 8 minutes or until lightly browned. Cool on cookie sheets 2 minutes; remove to wire racks, and cool completely.
Yield: about 3 dozen cookies

Holiday Cooking Club

Friendship is the only requirement for joining this social club. A "cooking club" event encourages each individual or couple to get involved by preparing a part of the meal. Having several cooks guarantees a night of lively conversation, abundant laughter, and lots of flavorful food! We're providing a blend of casual and formal recipes, so your group can create a meal that's perfectly suited to everyone's taste.

Regional fare, such as zesty **Crab Quesadillas with Poblano Cream** or sweet Sangria, make an interesting addition to traditional holiday dishes.

How To Roast Peppers

Broil peppers on all sides until "blistered."

Peel peppers and discard skin.

Remove and discard stems and seeds.

Everyone who samples **Crab Quesadillas with Poblano Cream** will think they've been transported to a south-of-the-border seaside café. If you use a panini press instead of a skillet, you'll reduce cooking time, and you won't have to turn the quesadillas!

SANGRIA

- 1 lime, cut into slices
- 1 lemon, cut into slices
- 1 orange, cut into slices
- 1 Granny Smith apple, cored and cut into slices
- 1 (750-milliliter) bottle dry red wine
- 1 (12-ounce) can lemon-lime carbonated beverage
  Garnish: orange and lime slices

Fill a pitcher with citrus slices; press fruit with the back of a spoon to release juice. Add apple slices and wine. Chill until serving time. Just before serving, add lemon-lime beverage. Serve over ice. Top each serving with an orange or a lime slice.
Yield: 2 quarts punch

FRESH TOMATILLO SALSA

- 2 Anaheim chile peppers
- 12 tomatillos (1 pound)
- 2 fresh serrano chile peppers, cut in half
- $1/2$ cup coarsely chopped onion
- 1 garlic clove, minced
- $1/4$ cup coarsely chopped fresh cilantro
- 1 teaspoon olive oil
- 1 teaspoon lime juice
- $1/4$ teaspoon salt

Place Anaheim chiles on an aluminum foil-lined baking sheet. Broil 5 inches from heat (with electric oven door partially open) about 5 minutes on each side or until peppers look blistered. Place roasted peppers in a heavy-duty zip-top plastic bag; seal and let stand 10 minutes to loosen skins. Peel peppers; remove and discard seeds. Coarsely chop peppers, and set aside. Pulse tomatillos in a food processor until coarsely chopped. Add roasted pepper, serrano chile peppers, and next 3 ingredients; pulse until diced (do not puree). Pour into a serving bowl. Stir in oil, lime juice, and salt until well blended. Cover and chill at least 1 hour.
Yield: 2 cups salsa

CRAB QUESADILLAS WITH POBLANO CREAM

Each quesadilla has as much calcium as one glass of milk.

  2   fresh poblano chiles (about $^{1}/_{2}$ pound)
  3   ounces cream cheese, softened (about $^{1}/_{3}$ cup)
$^{1}/_{4}$ cup sour cream
  1   tablespoon fresh lime juice
  1   teaspoon bottled minced roasted garlic
  1   pound lump crabmeat, shell pieces removed
$1^{1}/_{4}$ cups (5 ounces) shredded Monterey Jack cheese
$^{1}/_{2}$ cup sliced green onions
  1   teaspoon ground coriander
$^{1}/_{4}$ teaspoon salt
  6   flour tortillas (8 inch dia.)
      Butter-flavored cooking spray
$1^{1}/_{2}$ cups chopped tomato

Cut chiles in half lengthwise, and discard stems, seeds, and membranes. Place chile halves, skin side up, on a foil-lined baking sheet, and flatten with hand. Broil 15 minutes or until chiles are blackened. Place in a zip-top plastic bag; seal bag, and let stand 5 minutes. Peel chiles. Place roasted chiles, cream cheese, and next 3 ingredients in a food processor; process until smooth, scraping sides of processor bowl twice. Reserve 6 tablespoons Poblano Cream to top quesadillas. Combine remaining Poblano Cream, crabmeat, and next 4 ingredients in a medium bowl; stir until blended. Spread about $^{1}/_{2}$ cup crab mixture over half of 1 tortilla; fold tortilla in half to cover filling. Repeat procedure with remaining crab mixture and tortillas. Cover quesadillas with a slightly damp towel to keep them from drying out. Coat a large nonstick skillet with cooking spray, and place over medium heat until hot. Add 2 quesadillas, and cook 2 minutes on each side or until browned. Remove quesadillas from skillet; set aside, and keep warm. Repeat procedure with remaining quesadillas. Cut each quesadilla in half. Top each serving with $^{1}/_{4}$ cup chopped tomato and 1 tablespoon reserved Poblano Cream.

Yield: 6 servings

Note: A panini press or other indoor grill may be used to cook the quesadillas for 3 minutes or until tortillas are golden brown. For Shrimp Quesadillas, substitute 1 pound cooked, peeled, medium shrimp, coarsely chopped.

Avocado Citrus Salad

For a complete meal, top with grilled chicken strips or canned albacore tuna.

- 3 tablespoons cider vinegar
- 2 tablespoons vegetable oil
- 1 tablespoon sugar
- 1/4 teaspoon salt
- 8 cups torn salad greens
- 2 oranges, peeled and sectioned
- 1 large grapefruit, peeled and sectioned
- 1 pear, peeled and thinly sliced
- 2 ripe avocados, peeled and sliced
- 1 cup seedless red grapes
- 2 tablespoons chopped walnuts, toasted (optional)

Whisk together vinegar, oil, sugar, and salt; set aside. Place greens in a large bowl. Add orange and grapefruit sections, pear, avocados, and grapes. Drizzle with dressing, tossing gently to coat. Sprinkle with walnuts, if desired. Serve immediately.

Yield: 6 servings

Butternut Squash Soup

- 2 cans (14 ounces each) chicken broth
- 1 small Granny Smith apple, peeled and quartered
- 4 cups (about 1 1/2 pounds) butternut squash, peeled and cut into 1-inch cubes
- 1 cup chopped onion
- 1 teaspoon sugar
- 1/2 teaspoon salt
- 1/2 teaspoon curry powder
- 1/4 teaspoon pepper
- 1/2 cup whipping cream
  Toasted squash seeds (optional; see Note)

In a 3 1/2-quart electric slow cooker, combine chicken broth, apple, squash, onion, sugar, salt, curry powder, and pepper. Cover and cook on HIGH 4 hours. Spoon half of mixture into a blender. With center cap of blender lid removed, process soup, in batches, at low speed until smooth. Pour soup into a tureen or serving bowl; stir in cream. Serve with toasted squash seeds, if desired.

Yield: about 7 1/2 cups soup

Note: To toast squash seeds, place cleaned seeds on a lightly greased jellyroll pan. Bake at 275° for 20 minutes, stirring once.

A casual get-together to share the preparation of a meal can be the perfect opportunity for discovering new dishes. **Avocado Citrus Salad** is a festive mélange of salad greens, fruit, and nuts.

Even traditional holiday fare becomes a new sensation when you cook it outdoors with mesquite — Chili-Spiced Smoked Turkey Breast is sure to garner high praise for its chef.

CHILI-SPICED SMOKED TURKEY BREAST

You don't need a smoker — any covered grill will give the same effect. Simply place the turkey breast on the cool side of the grill, and use soaked wood chips.

- ¹/₄ cup fresh lime juice
- 2 tablespoons olive oil
- 2 teaspoons unsweetened cocoa
- 2 teaspoons paprika
- 2 teaspoons brown sugar
- 1 teaspoon salt
- 1 teaspoon dried oregano
- 1 teaspoon chili powder
- 1 teaspoon dried thyme
- 2 garlic cloves, minced
- 1 whole turkey breast (about 6 pounds)
- 2 cups mesquite chips
  Cooking spray

Combine lime juice, oil, cocoa, paprika, brown sugar, salt, oregano, chili powder, thyme, and garlic in a small saucepan; bring to a boil. Remove from heat; cool. Combine lime juice mixture and turkey in a large zip-top plastic bag. Seal and marinate in refrigerator 2 hours. Soak wood chips in water at least 30 minutes. Drain well.

Preheat gas grill to medium-hot (350° to 400°) using both burners. Turn left burner off. Place wood chips in a disposable foil pan or a foil packet pierced with holes on grill over right burner. Remove turkey from marinade; discard marinade. Place turkey, skin side up, on grill rack coated with cooking spray over left burner. Cover and cook 1¹/₂ hours. Turn turkey over; cook 15 minutes or until meat thermometer registers 170°. Remove turkey from grill. Cover loosely with foil, and let stand at least 10 minutes before carving. Discard skin.
Yield: 8 to 10 servings

Sweet potatoes are often a part of holiday feasts, but instead of being gooey with sugar or marshmallows, **Roasted Rosemary-Garlic Sweet Potatoes** are refreshingly savory.

ROASTED ROSEMARY-GARLIC SWEET POTATOES

- 5 large sweet potatoes, peeled and cut into 1½-inch chunks (about 4½ pounds)
- 10 large garlic cloves, crushed
- ⅓ cup olive oil
- 1 tablespoon chopped fresh rosemary
- 1 teaspoon salt
- ½ teaspoon pepper
  Garnish: fresh rosemary sprigs

Toss together sweet potatoes, garlic, and olive oil in a large, lightly greased roasting pan; sprinkle with chopped rosemary, salt, and pepper. Bake, uncovered, at 450° for 30 to 35 minutes, stirring every 10 minutes or until potatoes are tender and brown. Garnish, if desired.
Yield: 10 servings
Note: This is a great dish to prepare a day ahead and store overnight in a zip-top plastic bag, then bake when ready.

SAUTÉ OF MIXED VEGETABLES

Chayote are small, green, pear-shaped squash that are called mirlitons in Louisiana. They're mild in flavor and sometimes split, stuffed, and baked like acorn squash.

- 2 cups cauliflower florets
- 2 cups (1-inch) sliced green beans
- 1½ cups diagonally sliced carrot
- 1½ cups cubed peeled chayote (about ½ pound)
- 1 tablespoon vegetable oil
- 1 cup chopped onion
- 1 cup chopped green bell pepper
- 2 garlic cloves, finely chopped
- ¾ teaspoon salt
- ½ teaspoon ground cumin
- ¼ teaspoon pepper
- ⅓ cup chopped fresh cilantro

Bring 3 quarts of water to a boil in a large Dutch oven. Add the cauliflower, and cook for 3 minutes. Add green beans, carrot, and chayote; cover and cook an additional 4 minutes. Drain and rinse under cold water; drain well, and set aside. Heat oil in pan over medium heat. Add onion, bell pepper, and garlic; cover and cook for 8 minutes or until tender, stirring occasionally. Add cauliflower mixture, salt, cumin, and pepper; cover and cook an additional 5 minutes or until thoroughly heated. Remove from heat, and stir in cilantro.
Yield: 8 servings
Note: Zucchini can be substituted for chayote, if desired.

COFFEE-KAHLÚA GRANITA

¹/₂	cup sugar
1	cup water
1	stick cinnamon (3 inches long)
2¹/₂	cups brewed coffee
¹/₂	cup Kahlúa
	Garnish: cinnamon sticks

Combine sugar, water, and cinnamon stick in a saucepan; bring to a boil, stirring until sugar dissolves. Cool to room temperature. Discard cinnamon. Combine syrup, coffee, and Kahlúa; chill. Pour mixture into two freezer trays or a 9-inch square pan; freeze until almost firm, stirring occasionally. Let stand at room temperature about 10 minutes before serving. Scrape and shave granita with a fork until fluffy. Garnish with cinnamon sticks. Serve immediately.
Yield: 8 cups granita

Every memorable evening should end with coffee, especially when it's icy **Coffee-Kahlúa Granita**. Cinnamon gives this sweet treat an unexpected flavor boost.

Cooking Clubs:
Sharing the Fun All Year

Finding an evening to relax and visit with friends can be difficult throughout the year, not just during the holidays. Meeting at a restaurant is one solution, but precious time that should be used for visiting often gets gobbled up by a long wait for a table or a noisy environment that makes normal conversation impossible.

If you would like to make better use of your time with friends, consider forming a cooking club. Club members take turns hosting dinners, and everyone cooks for each meal. It's a fun way to shake off stress and spend every minute visiting, while no one feels exhausted from having to prepare an entire dinner.

Organizing your cooking club is easy. First, determine how often you and your friends would like to meet. Some groups find that one meeting per month is manageable for even the busiest members. And most groups limit their number to six or eight people to keep planning easy.

Your club will also want to decide how much of the food preparation is done at the host's home. Maybe everyone enjoys the bustle of all the members cooking their dishes at the same time. Or you may choose to have the host cook the entrée while remaining members bring completed dishes. No matter where the food is cooked, preparing the ingredients beforehand will save time.

Other considerations are whether or not a budget should be established and if alcohol will be served. The opinions of all members are important, and everyone should be comfortable with the decisions that are made.

One thing all cooking clubs seem to agree on is that no one has to be a gourmet chef to join in the fun. It really doesn't matter whether the food is an old favorite or something new and exotic, because friendship is the true focus of each meal … sharing good food is just a pleasant way to keep in touch.

in·a twinkling

Think you need a lot of time to create a delicious holiday dinner? Not so! A handful of ingredients added to ready-made dishes will quickly yield festive foods, as well as plenty of goodies for snacking!

What's easier than apple pie? Cornmeal Streusel Apple Pie! A sweet and crumbly topping is all it takes to add homemade flavor to a "store-bought" dessert.

CORNMEAL STREUSEL APPLE PIE

Dress up a storebought fruit pie with our Southern cornmeal streusel. Your guests will think the whole thing's from scratch, especially since you'll serve it from your own pieplate.

- ¹/₂ cup chopped walnuts
- ¹/₂ cup firmly packed light brown sugar
- 3 tablespoons all-purpose flour
- 3 tablespoons yellow cornmeal
- ³/₄ teaspoon ground cinnamon
- ¹/₄ teaspoon ground nutmeg
- ¹/₂ cup (2 ounces) shredded sharp Cheddar cheese
- ¹/₃ cup unsalted butter, slightly softened
- 1 frozen deep-dish apple pie (3 pounds, 1 ounce)

Stir together first 6 ingredients in a medium bowl; stir in cheese. Gently work in butter with fingertips until mixture forms large crumbs. Cover and chill 30 minutes.

Meanwhile, remove frozen pie from aluminum pieplate and place in an ungreased 10" deep-dish pieplate. Cut slits in top crust according to package directions. Bake, uncovered, at 375° for 50 minutes. Remove from oven. Sprinkle cornmeal streusel over pie, mounding slightly in center. Bake, uncovered, 20 to 25 more minutes or until browned and bubbly. Cool in pieplate on a wire rack at least 30 minutes before serving.
Yield: one 10" pie

TURKEY AND GORGONZOLA SALAD

- 8 ounces deli-style turkey, cubed
- 1 Gala apple, cored and thinly sliced
- ¹/₂ cup chopped red onion
- 1 package (5 ounces) spring greens salad mix
- ¹/₄ cup pecans, toasted
- ¹/₃ cup (1.3 ounces) crumbled Gorgonzola cheese
- ¹/₄ teaspoon freshly ground black pepper
- ¹/₂ cup frozen apple juice concentrate, thawed
- ¹/₄ cup balsamic vinegar
- 1¹/₂ teaspoons dark sesame oil

Combine first 3 ingredients in a medium bowl; toss well. Place 1¹/₂ cups spring greens on each of 4 plates. Top evenly with turkey mixture; sprinkle with pecans, cheese, and pepper. Combine apple juice concentrate, vinegar, and oil; stir well with a whisk. Spoon about 3 tablespoons dressing over each serving.
Yield: 4 servings
Notes: If you're unable to find the spring greens salad mix, use 6 cups of any type of salad greens. You can also use blue cheese instead of the Gorgonzola. We preferred the sweet flavor and crisp texture of the Gala apple for this salad. Braeburn or Fuji apples would be good substitutes.

You'll never fill salad plates faster than when you use packaged salad mix to prepare **Turkey and Gorgonzola Salad.** Crisp apples, crunchy pecans, and tangy cheese make this dish a party favorite.

TOASTED POLENTA ROUNDS

Look for tubes of polenta in the refrigerated produce section of the supermarket.

- 1 tube (16 ounces) of polenta, cut into 8 slices
  Olive oil-flavored cooking spray
- 2 tablespoons preshredded fresh Parmesan cheese
- 1 teaspoon Italian seasoning

Preheat oven to 450°. Coat both sides of polenta slices with cooking spray, and place on a baking sheet. Sprinkle evenly with cheese and seasoning. Bake at 450° for 20 to 25 minutes or until golden.
Yield: 4 servings

Toasted Polenta Rounds are incredibly simple, wonderfully savory, and ready to serve in just minutes. Ditto for the **Cheddar Mashed Potatoes** — everyone's favorite side dish goes from freezer to table in a flash.

CHEDDAR MASHED POTATOES

Garlic and herb cheese spread and Cheddar cheese double the flavor of this familiar side dish.

- 1 package (22 ounces) frozen mashed potatoes
- 2¹/₃ cups milk
- ¹/₃ cup spreadable cheese with garlic and herbs (such as Alouette)
- ¹/₂ cup (2 ounces) shredded sharp Cheddar cheese
- ¹/₄ teaspoon salt
- ¹/₈ teaspoon pepper

Prepare mashed potatoes according to package directions, using milk. Stir in remaining ingredients.
Yield: 5 servings
Note: Vary the flavor of cheese spread and you have a new recipe. Other cheese spread flavors include Sundried Tomato and Basil, Vegetable Garden, and Lite Herbs.

It won't be just the kids who make the **Peanut Butter and Jelly Cookies** disappear. The sweet treats use cookie dough from the grocery store, so it's easy to bake extras in short order. And you can satisfy hearty appetites with **Chicken and Wild Rice Casserole** in less than an hour!

PEANUT BUTTER AND JELLY COOKIES

1 (18-ounce) package refrigerated peanut butter cookie dough
1½ cups strawberry jam

Preheat the oven to 350°. Cut dough into ¼-inch slices and roll into balls; flatten sliced dough in a crisscross pattern with a floured fork. Bake at 350° for 9 to 10 minutes or until lightly browned. Cool 1 minute on cookie sheets; remove to wire racks to cool. Spread jam on bottoms of half the cookies; top with remaining cookies.

Yield: 18 sandwich cookies

CHICKEN AND WILD RICE CASSEROLE

For added convenience, pick up a freshly roasted whole chicken from the grocery store deli.

1 (6.2-ounce) package fast-cooking long-grain and wild rice mix
2 cups low-sodium chicken broth
1 package (8 ounces) fresh mushroom slices
3 cups chopped cooked chicken
½ cup Italian dressing
1 container (8 ounces) sour cream

Cook rice in a large saucepan according to package directions, using 2 cups chicken broth instead of water. Add mushrooms before the last 5 minutes. Stir in chicken, dressing, and sour cream; spoon into a lightly greased 2-quart baking dish. Bake at 325° for 30 minutes or until thoroughly heated. Let stand 10 minutes.

Yield: 6 servings

CHEESECAKE SAMPLER

1 frozen cheesecake (2 pounds)
  Cheesecake Toppings (suggestions follow)

Thaw cheesecake. Cut into 8 wedges; top each slice with desired Cheesecake Toppings.
Yield: 8 servings

CHEESECAKE TOPPINGS

Peppermint Cheesecake: Spoon one can ready-made cream cheese frosting into a microwave-safe bowl. Microwave at HIGH for 30 seconds or until almost melted and stirrable. Combine frosting and crushed peppermint candy; stir well. Spread over slice. Place whole peppermint candies around crust edge.

Black-and-White Cheesecake: Spoon one can each ready-made chocolate and cream cheese frostings into separate microwave-safe bowls. Microwave each at HIGH 20 seconds or just until soft and pipeable. Spoon frostings into separate heavy-duty, zip-top plastic bags. Seal; snip a tiny hole in the corner of each bag. Pipe chocolate frosting in a zigzag fashion over the slice. Pipe cream cheese frosting over chocolate frosting in the opposite direction. Pipe additional chocolate frosting over cream cheese frosting. Place chocolate-covered coffee beans on crust edge, using chocolate frosting to secure in place.

Walnut Cheesecake: Spoon walnuts-in-syrup ice cream topping over slice.

Raspberry Cheesecake: Brush melted seedless raspberry jam over slice. Arrange fresh raspberries over slice; brush lightly with additional melted jam.

Your holiday guests will count themselves very fortunate in their host when you serve a tempting Cheesecake Sampler. With luscious toppings of peppermint, chocolate, walnuts in syrup, and raspberry, everyone will enjoy deciding which to try first.

toast
The New Year

Whether you choose to end the holiday season with a light collation of finger foods or a large and hearty breakfast, any combination of these satisfying recipes will get your New Year off to a delicious start.

Greet the New Year with tall glasses of Holiday Punch, and provide plenty of elegant Smoked Salmon Canapés for nibbling.

Frozen puff pastry makes it easy to create a platterful of light and flaky Fig and Gruyère Palmiers.

HOLIDAY PUNCH

Chill this pink punch in a wine bottle encased in an ice block of berries and greenery.

- 1 bottle (750-milliliters) white Zinfandel (see Note)
  Holly leaves and berries or pepperberries
- 1 quart distilled water
- 1 jar (10 ounces) maraschino cherries with stems, undrained
- 3 cans (6 ounces each) pineapple juice
- 1 bottle (64 ounces) cranberry-cherry juice drink
- 1 can (12 ounces) frozen lemonade concentrate, thawed and undiluted
- 2 bottles (750 milliliters each) champagne, chilled (see Note)

For ice cylinder, pour wine into a pitcher; cover and chill. Rinse out wine bottle, and remove label, using warm soapy water. Rinse out a half-gallon juice carton or milk carton; cut off top. Place wine bottle in carton. (Do not cork or cap bottle, or it may break during freezing.) Tape neck of bottle to top of carton with masking tape to center and secure it. Arrange holly leaves and berries between bottle and carton, using a long wooden skewer or handle of a wooden spoon to position leaves and berries. Add distilled water to 1/2 inch below top of carton. Freeze at least 8 hours, repositioning leaves and berries as water starts to freeze.

Drain cherries over a large bowl, reserving juice. Reserve cherries to garnish each serving, if desired. Add pineapple juice, cranberry-cherry juice drink, and lemonade concentrate to cherry juice; stir well, and chill.

Remove carton with wine bottle from freezer. Pour cold water into bottle. Dip carton into a sinkful of cold water. (Ice and bottle may crack if warm water is used.) Tear carton away from ice cylinder; remove bottle. Empty water from wine bottle.

Combine chilled wine, juice mixture, and champagne. Pour punch through a funnel into bottle, refilling as needed. Place ice cylinder upright in a large bowl of crushed ice to slow the melting; insert bottle filled with punch. To serve, gently slip bottle from frozen cylinder (catch drips with a linen towel).

Yield: 2 1/4 gallons punch

Note: For nonalcoholic punch, substitute 3 (25.4-ounce) bottles sparkling white grape juice for wine and champagne.

SMOKED SALMON CANAPÉS

Pair these upscale open-faced sandwiches with Pinot Noir. It complements salmon well.

- 4 ounces (1/2 of an 8-ounce package) cream cheese, softened
- 1/4 cup sour cream
- 1 tablespoon honey
- 1/2 teaspoon freshly ground pepper
- 1/4 teaspoon salt
- 24 slices party rye or pumpernickel bread
- 12 ounces smoked salmon
- 48 very thin slices cucumber
  Minced purple onion
  Freshly ground pepper
  Garnish: fresh dill, separated into tiny sprigs

Combine first 5 ingredients in a bowl; beat at low speed of an electric mixer until thoroughly blended. Cut each bread slice diagonally in half. Separate salmon into very thin slices (smoked salmon should separate naturally into slivers). Cut salmon into 48 pieces. Spread 1/2 teaspoon cream cheese mixture onto each piece of bread. Roll a cucumber slice inside each salmon piece; place over cream cheese spread on bread. Dollop 1/2 teaspoon cream cheese mixture over salmon. Sprinkle with onion and pepper; garnish, if desired.

Yield: 4 dozen canapés

FIG AND GRUYÈRE PALMIERS

Fig preserves and Gruyère cheese taste great together in this easy French pastry called a palmier. Be sure to line your baking sheets with parchment paper; it makes clean-up so easy. A light and slightly sweet Riesling or Gewürztraminer is our pick for these pastries.

  1 package (17.3 ounces) frozen puff pastry, thawed
  2 cups (8 ounces) shredded Gruyère cheese
 ²/₃ cup fig preserves, melted

Roll one puff pastry sheet into a 14 x 10-inch rectangle. Sprinkle with 1 cup Gruyère cheese. Roll each long side, jellyroll fashion, to meet in center. Repeat procedure with remaining puff pastry sheet and cheese. Cut each roll into ¹/₂-inch slices. Place slices on parchment paper-lined baking sheets; spread with melted preserves. Bake at 400° for 8 to 10 minutes or until golden. Serve warm.
Yield: 56 appetizers
Note: You can make these pastries ahead and freeze the uncut, unbaked rolls. Wrap rolls in heavy-duty plastic wrap, and freeze. To serve, let rolls stand at room temperature 10 minutes before slicing. Spread with preserves and bake as above.

TRADITIONAL EGGS BENEDICT

  4 large eggs
  8 slices (¹/₂ ounce each) Canadian bacon
     Vegetable cooking spray
  2 English muffins, split and toasted
     Hollandaise Sauce (recipe follows)
     Coarsely ground pepper
     Paprika

Pour water to a depth of 3" in a large saucepan; bring to a boil, reduce heat, and maintain at a light simmer. Add ¹/₂ teaspoon vinegar. Break eggs and slip into water one at a time, as close as possible to surface of water. Simmer 3 to 5 minutes or to desired degree of doneness; remove with a slotted spoon and trim edges, if desired. Cook bacon in skillet coated with cooking spray over medium heat until thoroughly heated, turning once. Drain on paper towels. Place 2 bacon slices on each muffin half. Top each with a poached egg, and drizzle evenly with Hollandaise Sauce. Sprinkle with pepper and paprika; serve immediately.
Yield: 2 servings

HOLLANDAISE SAUCE

  4 large egg yolks
  2 tablespoons fresh lemon juice
  1 cup butter, melted
 ¹/₄ teaspoon salt

Whisk yolks in top of a double boiler; gradually whisk in lemon juice. Place over hot water (do not boil). Add butter, ¹/₃ cup at a time, whisking until smooth; whisk in salt. Cook, whisking constantly, 10 minutes or until thickened and a thermometer registers 160°. Serve immediately.
Yield: 1¹/₂ cups sauce

For an intimate celebration you'll always remember, prepare an early breakfast of Traditional Eggs Benedict and Hollandaise Sauce. It's an elegant way to start your New Year.

CHICKEN-PECAN QUICHE

We loved this Southern take on quiche with its Cheddar cheese, chicken, pecan topping, and savory Cheddar crust so much we gave it our highest rating.

- 1 cup all-purpose flour
- 1 cup (4 ounces) shredded sharp Cheddar cheese
- 3/4 cup chopped pecans
- 1/2 teaspoon salt
- 1/4 teaspoon paprika
- 1/3 cup vegetable oil
- 1 cup sour cream
- 1/2 cup chicken broth
- 1/4 cup mayonnaise
- 3 large eggs, lightly beaten
- 2 cups chopped cooked chicken
- 1/2 cup (2 ounces) shredded sharp Cheddar cheese
- 1/4 cup minced fresh onion
- 1/2 teaspoon dried dillweed
- 3 drops of hot sauce
- 1/4 cup pecan halves

Combine first 5 ingredients in a medium bowl; stir well. Add oil; stir well. Firmly press mixture on bottom and up sides of a 9" deep-dish pieplate. Bake at 350° for 12 minutes. Cool completely. Beat sour cream, broth, mayonnaise, and eggs until smooth. Stir in chicken and next 4 ingredients. Pour chicken mixture over prepared crust. Arrange pecan halves over chicken mixture. Bake at 350° for 45 minutes or until set. Let stand 10 minutes before serving.

Yield: one 9" quiche

Note: You can substitute turkey or a 9-ounce package of frozen diced cooked chicken for the chopped cooked chicken.

Chicken-Pecan Quiche is a warm and pleasing dish that will generate many requests for the recipe. To save preparation time, make the Cheddar crust before your guests arrive.

SAVORY SAUSAGE-SWISS MUFFINS

Reheat leftover muffins in the microwave; one muffin heats in 20 to 30 seconds at HIGH.

- ½ pound mild or spicy ground pork sausage
- 1¾ cups biscuit mix
- ½ cup (2 ounces) shredded Swiss cheese
- ¾ teaspoon ground sage
- ¼ teaspoon dried thyme
- 1 large egg, lightly beaten
- ¾ cup milk

Brown sausage in a skillet over medium heat, stirring until it crumbles. Drain well. Combine sausage, biscuit mix, and next 3 ingredients in a bowl; make a well in center of mixture. Combine egg and milk; add to dry ingredients, stirring just until dry ingredients are moistened. Spoon batter into greased muffin pans, filling two-thirds full. Bake at 375° for 22 minutes or until golden. Serve warm. Store leftovers in refrigerator.

Yield: 1 dozen muffins

Breakfast should always be this easy — Savory Sausage-Swiss Muffins are as tasty as the name implies, and any leftovers will make a great "on-the-go" breakfast. Before the New Year's resolutions begin, be sure to serve luscious Chocolate-Dipped Strawberries.

CHOCOLATE-DIPPED STRAWBERRIES

- 2 quarts fresh strawberries
- 2 cups (12 ounces) semisweet chocolate morsels
- ½ cup whipping cream

Rinse strawberries, and pat completely dry with paper towels (chocolate will not stick to wet strawberries). Insert toothpicks; set aside. Microwave chocolate morsels and whipping cream in a 1-quart microwave-safe bowl at MEDIUM (50% power) 3½ minutes. Stir until smooth. Hold strawberries by toothpicks, and dip into melted chocolate, allowing excess to drip. Place on wax paper, and let stand until chocolate hardens. Chill 1 hour.

Yield: 5 dozen strawberries

Project Instructions

Christmas decorating has never been easier! Our easy-to-follow instructions guide you, step-by-step, as you craft handmade projects that will fill your home with customized appeal. Refer to the General Instructions on page 184 for extra "how-to" tips and techniques.

Radiant Stars

BEAD-TRIMMED CANDLESTICKS
(shown on page 10)

You will need The Ultimate! glue by Crafter's Pick™, beaded trim; brass candlestick with etched and beveled hurricane globe; 1/8" dia. gold cording; beading needle and thread; green, gold, yellow, and red seed beads, 8mm green beads, 4mm and 8mm gold beads; and four Beaded Dangles (page 121).

1. Glue a length of beaded trim around candlestick.
2. Glue two lengths of cording to flange of trim.
3. Measure around cording on candlestick, then cut a length of thread twice the determined measurement.
4. Alternating green and gold seed beads, string approximately 15 green seed, then one gold seed bead. Repeat pattern, spacing evenly to fit around candlestick.

5. (*Note:* Refer to Fig. 1 for Step 5.) For each tassel, knot one end of a 7" length of thread around one gold seed bead. Thread seventeen yellow seed, one 8mm green, one red seed, two 4mm gold, one 8mm gold bead, and one Beaded Dangle onto thread; double back through 8mm gold bead and one 4mm gold bead. Thread one 4mm gold, one red seed, one 8mm green, then seventeen yellow seed beads onto thread. Knot remaining end of thread through next gold seed bead; trim excess thread.

Fig. 1

6. Using a beading needle to hold beads in place until glue dries, glue one 4mm gold bead at each point and intersection of bevels on globe.

GOLD BEADED TASSEL
(shown on page 11)

You will need 1/16" dia. and 1/8" dia. gold cording, tacky glue, and 2 1/2"-long and 1 1/2"-long beaded trim.

1. For hanger, cut a 7" length of 1/16" dia. cording; fold in half and knot ends together.
2. Using glue to hold trim in place, wrap a 7" length of 2 1/2"-long trim around hanger, then wrap a 3 1/2" length of 1 1/2"-long trim around flange of 2 1/2"-long trim.
3. Starting at top of tassel, winding downward, and using glue to hold cording in place, wrap 1/8" dia. cording around flange of trim.

CHENILLE TASSEL
(shown on page 11)

You will need 10 yds. chenille yarn, 5" square of cardboard, tacky glue, and beaded trim.

1. Wrap 9 yds. of yarn around cardboard square.
2. Slide an 11" length of yarn under all strands at one end of square; knot tightly around yarn, then knot ends together to form hanger (Fig. 1).

Fig. 1

3. Referring to Fig. 2, cut yarn at opposite end of square.

Fig. 2

4. Wrap and glue a length of trim around top of tassel, then glue a length of yarn around flange of trim.

STAMPED MIRROR ORNAMENTS
(shown on page 11)

For each mirror, you will need a small mirror (we used a 2" x 3" oval, 2" dia. circle, and 1¼" square), self-adhesive felt; clear gloss permanent enamel glaze, bronze pigment powder, disposable bowl, foam brush, rubber stamp, ³⁄₁₆"w copper foil tape, 20-gauge gold wire, wire cutters and needle-nose pliers, assorted beads, and one or more Beaded Dangles (page 121).

1. Draw around mirror on paper side of felt; cut out and set aside.
2. Mix one part glaze with one part pigment powder in disposable bowl, then brush mixture on desired rubber stamp. Stamp mirror, then allow to dry.
3. Adhere foil tape along front and edges of mirror.
4. Cut a 10" length of wire. Bead a 3" – 4" loop at one end of wire, twisting end of wire around itself to secure loop in place.
5. With loop close to bottom of mirror, arrange remaining wire along center back of mirror; adhere felt shape to back of mirror, holding wire in place.
6. Add additional beads to wire at top of ornament; make a curlicue in wire above beads to secure, then form a hook for hanger. If necessary, trim excess wire.
7. Add Beaded Dangles to bottom loop as desired.

METAL STAND
(shown on pages 9 and 11)

You will need black and light grey acrylic paint, paintbrushes, large brass urn, soft cloth, gold metallic finish, masking tape, length of hard plastic pipe the height of urn and slightly larger than tree trunk, quick-drying concrete mix, hot glue gun, plastic foam pieces, sheet moss, and an artificial Christmas tree.

1. Working in small sections, paint urn black, then wipe away paint with a soft cloth; repeat with grey paint as desired.
2. Follow manufacturer's instructions to apply rub-on finish to urn as desired.
3. Use tape to form a grid across top of urn to hold pipe in place at center of urn.
4. Follow manufacturer's instructions to mix concrete. Fill bottom 4" of urn with concrete and allow to set; remove tape.
5. Using glue to hold foam together, fill remainder of urn with foam pieces, then cover foam with moss.
6. Place tree in pipe.

Tip For a two-sided Stamped Mirror Ornament, follow Steps 2 and 3 to make an additional mirror and glue to back of ornament.

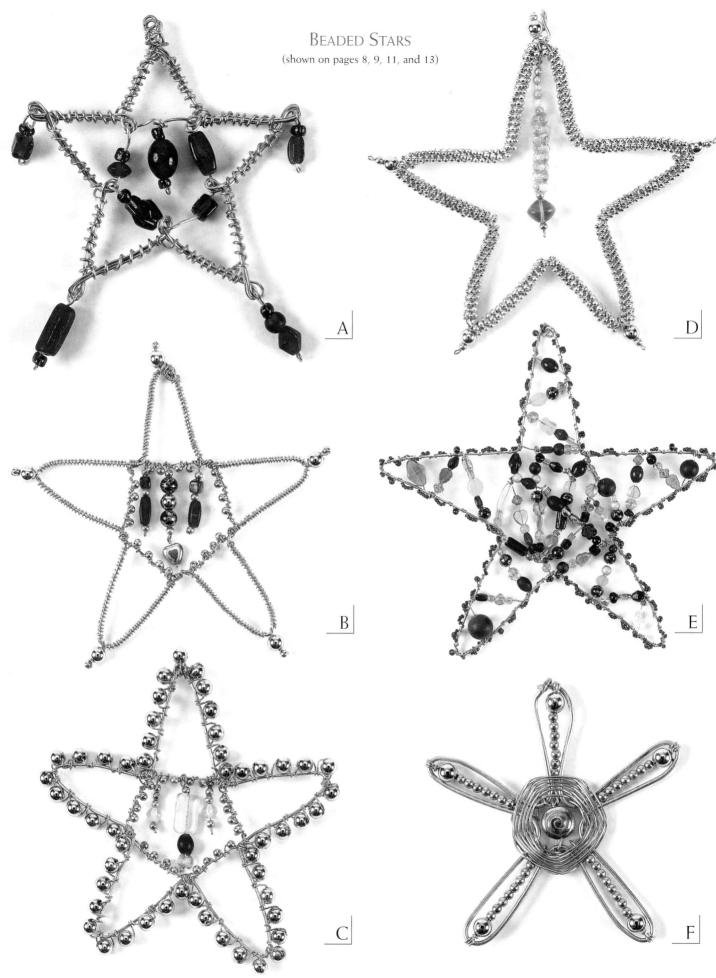

BEADED STARS
(shown on pages 8, 9, 11, and 13)

A

B

C

D

E

F

You will need wire cutters, needle nose pliers (to hold wire), and round-nose jewelry pliers (to make loops and curlicues in wire), assorted glass beads (see specific Beaded Star instructions for any specific beads).

Refer to Star Components, page 121, for all Beaded Star instructions.

Star A
You will also need 20-gauge gold jewelry wire and assorted glass beads.

Use 20-gauge gold wire for all steps.

1. Using small star pattern, page 164, follow Making a Jig for Wire Stars (page 120).
2. For star frame, beginning at top point on jig, refer to Fig. 1 to make a loop at top, then wrap wire around nails once; repeat two more times. Wrap wire ends around base of top loop to secure; clip wire ends. Remove nails from jig.

Fig. 1

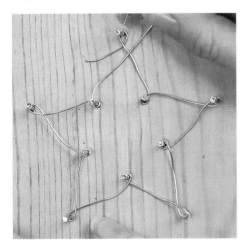

3. Add Center Support Wires for Small Beaded Stars, then follow Wrapped Wire to add wire around star frame. Add five Beaded Dangles and a Hanger.

Star B
You will need 16-gauge galvanized wire for star frame, 20-gauge gold jewelry wire, 4mm and 8mm gold round beads, and assorted glass beads.

1. Using medium star pattern, page 164, follow Making a Jig for Wire Stars (page 120).
2. Beginning at top point on jig, refer to Fig. 2 to make a loop at top, then wrap 16-gauge wire around nails. Thread, then bend end of wire through loop to secure; trim excess wire as needed. Remove nails from jig.

Fig. 2

3. (Note: Use 20-gauge wire for remaining steps.) Add Center Support Wires for Large Beaded Stars; using 4mm beads add Wrapped Beaded Wire to center-supports.
4. Add Wrapped Wire to star frame. Using 4mm and 8mm beads and an 18" length of wire instead of a 3" wire length, add Beaded Points.
5. Add three Beaded Dangles to top support wire, then add a Hanger.

Star C
You will need 16-gauge galvanized wire for star frame, 20-gauge gold jewelry wire, 4mm and 8mm gold round beads, and assorted glass beads.

1. Using medium star pattern, page 164, follow Making a Jig for Wire Stars (page 120).
2. Follow Step 2 of Star B, above.
3. (Note: Use 20-gauge wire for remaining steps.) Add Center Support Wires for Large Beaded Stars.
4. Using 4mm beads, add Wrapped Beaded Wire to center supports. Using 8mm beads, add Wrapped Beaded Wire to star frame.
5. Add three Beaded Dangles to top support wire, then add a Hanger.

Star D
You will need 16-gauge galvanized wire for star forms, 20-gauge gold jewelry wire, 4mm and 8mm round beads, 3 yds. of 3mm gold bead garland, and assorted beads.

Hint: For Step 4, place the bulk of the bead garland in a snack-size plastic bag to make it easier to handle when wrapping the star frame.

1. Using medium star pattern, page 164, follow Making a Jig for Wire Stars (page 120).
2. Follow Step 2 of Star B, this page.
3. Add Beaded Points.
4. (Note: Add a dot of glue to ends of garland to secure beads in place.) Using a short length of 20-gauge wire to secure ends of garland to star frame, wrap frame with garland.
5. Add a long Beaded Dangle and a Hanger.

(Beaded Stars continued on next page.)

Star E

(page 118)

You will need 16-gauge galvanized wire for star form, 20- and 24-gauge gold jewelry wire, assorted glass beads, assorted seed beads, and ribbon (optional).

1. Enlarge medium star pattern, page 164, 150%. Using enlarged star pattern, follow Making a Jig for Wire Stars (this page).
2. Follow Step 2 of Star B, page 119.
3. Using 20-gauge wire, add Center Support Wires for Large Beaded Stars, threading beads onto wire between each center point.
4. Using 24-gauge wire and seed beads, add Wrapped Beaded Wire to star frame.
5. Wrap and cross lengths of 24-gauge wire throughout star as desired, adding beads and curlicues to wire.
6. Add a Hanger or knot a length of ribbon to top point to hang star.

Star F

(page 118)

You will need 16-gauge galvanized wire for star form, 20-gauge gold jewelry wire, 13mm bead, and 4mm and 8mm gold round beads.

1. Using medium star pattern, page 164, follow Making a Jig for Wire Stars (this page).
2. Follow Step 2 of Star B, page 119.
3. Press wires together at center points and along points.
4. Attach one end of a 22" length of 20-gauge wire to one center point. Continue wrapping wire over one point and under the next point (around center of star) until all wire is wound. Secure end of wire to star frame.

5. Thread 13mm bead onto center of a 2½" length of 20-gauge wire. Wrap one end of wire around a center point of frame and remaining end around a woven wire on opposite side of star; wrap wire around itself to secure.
6. For each point, thread one end of a 3" length of 20-gauge wire through woven wires and wrap end around a center woven wire. Thread eight 4mm beads and one 8mm bead onto wire; wrap end of wire around outer point three times, then around itself just above 8mm bead to secure. Trim excess wire as needed.
7. Add a Hanger.

MAKING A JIG FOR WIRE STARS

You will need tracing paper (optional); tape; 4", 6", and 9" squares of ¾"-thick wood for small, medium, and large star jigs; 1½"-long finishing nails; drill; and a drill bit slightly larger than nails.

1. For each jig, trace or photocopy the star pattern indicated in the individual star instructions (page 119 and this page). Tape pattern to appropriately sized wooden piece. Tap a nail at each point on pattern (Fig. 1), then remove pattern.

Fig. 1

2. Drill holes, slightly larger than nails, straight down into wood at points, so nails fit snug but can be easily removed (Fig. 2). Insert nails into holes.

Fig. 2

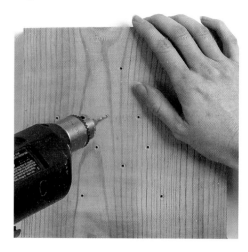

Tip Instead of inserting all the nails into the holes, then wrapping wire around them, try inserting the top nail, then placing the loop on it, before inserting the next nail. Continue inserting nails one at a time, until you have finished wrapping the wire around all nails.

STAR COMPONENTS

You will need gold jewelry wire, wire cutters, needle-nose pliers (to hold wire), and round-nose jewelry pliers (to make loops and curlicues in wire).

Refer to Beaded Star instructions (pages 119 – 120) for gauges of wire and beads to use for each star component.

Beaded Point

Thread a 4mm round bead onto center of a 3" length of wire; bend wire around bead, then thread wire ends through an 8mm bead. Wrap wire ends around point of star to secure. Trim excess wire as needed, then add a dot of clear-drying adhesive to secure the point.

Beaded Dangle

Thread desired beads onto a 3"-long headpin or eyepin OR cut a length of wire the desired length for dangle plus 2", then form a small loop at one end of wire; thread desired beads onto wire.

Wrap remaining end of pin or wire around a center support wire of a star or through the looped inner point of a star. Trim excess wire as needed.

Dangle Idea: Use a jump ring to add a charm to the bottom loop of a dangle.

Wrapped Wire

Beginning at a center point and using the same gauge or smaller gauge wire as star form, tightly wrap star form with wire. Trim excess wire as needed.

Wrapped Beaded Wire

Beginning at a center point and using a length of the same gauge or smaller gauge wire as star form, tightly wrap star form with wire, adding one or more beads as you wrap wire around star frame or a center support wire.

Center Support Wires for Small Beaded Stars

Wrap one end of a 10" length of wire around an inner loop; thread one or two beads onto wire. Cross over and thread wire through next inner loop; continue adding beads and threading wire through inner loops until complete. Wrap remaining end of wire around first inner loop to secure.

Center Support Wires for Large Beaded Stars

Wrap one end of a 12" length of wire three times around one center point; cross over and thread wire through next center point. Continue crossing and wrapping wire around center points until complete. Wrap remaining end of wire around first center point to secure.

Hanger

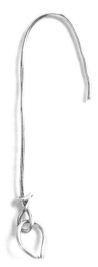

Wrap one end of a 3" length of wire around top point of star, then twist wire around itself to secure. Make a hook in remaining end of wire.

BEADED VOTIVE HOLDERS

(shown on page 13)

For each holder, you will need 8mm confetti beads; 4mm and 8mm gold round beads; 4mm green and 4mm red seed beads; 6mm red bead; 6mm red, 6mm yellow and 6mm green miracle beads; 20- and 26-gauge wire; wire cutters and needle-nose pliers; two 4" dia. gold metal rings; 5$^{1}/_{2}$"h x 4" dia. hurricane votive candleholder; heavy-duty thread; .015" dia. tiger tail wire, and Beaded Dangles (page 121).

1. Alternating confetti and 4mm gold beads, thread beads onto a 12$^{1}/_{2}$" length of 20-gauge wire. Connecting wire ends, form beaded wire into a circle. With beaded wire resting on ring for top of holder, use 26-gauge wire to wrap and attach beaded wire to ring.
2. With second ring pulled taut against bottom of holder and spacing evenly around holder, use three lengths of thread to connect top ring to bottom ring
3. Cut eight 13" lengths of tiger tail wire. Run center of one length of wire around top ring under beads, then matching ends, run both ends of wire through a confetti bead, then separate ends. Repeat for each wire, spacing evenly around ring.

4. Alternating 4mm gold and green seed beads, thread twelve beads onto each wire end; bend wire up to hold beads in place.
5. To join green beaded wires, thread neighboring wires through one 6mm red bead; bend wire up to hold beads in place.
6. Alternating red seed and 4mm gold beads, thread ten beads onto each wire end. Bend wire up to hold beads in place.
7. To complete beading, join two neighboring wires, then thread one confetti, one yellow miracle, one 8mm gold, one green miracle, then one confetti bead onto wire. Wrap wire ends around bottom ring, then thread ends through a crimp bead; crimp bead to secure wire around ring. Repeat until all neighboring wires have been joined.
8. Using two green seed and one 8mm gold bead and 20-gauge wire, attach a Beaded Dangle to wire above each crimp bead.
9. Clip and remove thread from holder.

Votive Diagram

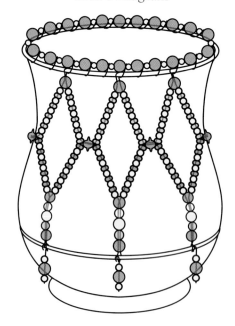

CHRISTMAS ANGEL

(shown on page 12)

You will need one 9"h and one 4"h gold bell-shaped metal lampshade frame with six ribs each; hot glue gun; gold beaded trim; wire cutters; 16- and 20-gauge wire; 4mm and 8mm gold beads and other assorted beads; 36 yds. of 3mm gold bead garland; one 5 yd. spool of 4mm gold bead garland, and two 9 ft. spools of 8mm gold bead garland; $^{1}/_{8}$" dia. armature wire; 6"h glass vase with opening same size as top of small frame; 4" dia. gold metal ring; 1$^{1}/_{2}$"w gold wire-edged ribbon; removable tape; paper-backed fusible web; buckram (an open weave, very stiff fabric); gold organza with metallic motifs; $^{1}/_{8}$" dia. gold metallic gold cording; hole punch; red and gold acrylic paint; paintbrush; craft sponge; and 1"-long sequin pins.

Tip If you can't find gold lampshade frames, simply spray paint the ones you have gold.

Use a pressing cloth for all fusing. Use 20-gauge wire to secure garlands to frames as needed.

1. For large frame, glue flange of beaded trim along base of frame.
2. Cut an 11" length of 16-gauge wire to fit between each rib around frame. Secure one end of each wire to base of frame, then thread each wire length with assorted gold beads; secure remaining end of each wire to top of frame.
3. Winding between each beaded dangle on trim, wrap 3mm garland around base of frame. Glue ends on inside of base to secure.
4. Cut thirty-six 20"-lengths of 3mm garland. For each length, fold in half and lay center of strand over top of frame, then pull ends through loop (Fig. 1). Spacing evenly, attach six lengths between each rib; glue ends to inside bottom of frame.

Fig. 1

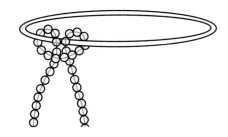

5. Measure around large frame just above base and add 1"; cut a length of 16-gauge wire the determined measurement. Thread wire with assorted beads, then securing beginning and ending wire ends around same rib at back, wrap beaded wire around frame.
6. Measure around large frame approximately ¹/₂" above beaded wire strand and add 1"; cut a length of 8mm garland the determined measurement. Beginning and ending at back, wrap garland around frame, threading garland over 3mm garland strands and behind gold beaded wire.

7. For small frame, beginning and ending at back, wrap 8mm garland around base of frame.
8. Follow Step 6 to add a beaded wire above base of small frame. Wrap remaining part of small frame with 3mm garland.
9. For arms, cut an 18"-length of armature wire and form it into a circle. Wrap one end of wire around a side rib at top of small frame; wrap remaining wire end around rib on opposite side of frame. Wrap arms with 8mm garland.
10. For head, lightly spray vase gold. Secure a length of 20-gauge wire around neck of vase. With open end of vase resting on frame, use lengths of 20-gauge wire to attach vase from wire around neck of vase to ribs.
11. For beaded necklace, measure around neck three times and add 2"; cut a length of wire the determined measurement. Thread wire with assorted beads, then wrap around neck three times; twist ends together at back to secure.
12. For garland necklace, wrap 8mm garland twice around neck just below beaded necklace.
13. (*Note:* Refer to Fig. 2 for this step.) For halo, cut two 9" pieces of 16-gauge wire. Wrap 3" of each piece in opposite directions around ring. Twist next 5" of wire together. Wrap ends around two ribs on small frame at back. Wrap halo with 4mm garland.

Fig. 2

14. For hair, cut five 16" lengths of ribbon. Overlap ribbon slightly along long edges, then run a basting stitch across center of ribbons; gather centers to approximately 1¹/₂"w. Glue hair to head along gathered area; arrange hair.
15. Enlarge wing pattern on page 164, 127%; make one additional copy. Cut out patterns, then tape together as indicated.
16. Follow Steps 1 – 3 of *Fusible Appliqués*, page 185, to make two appliqués from buckram and two appliqués from organza.
17. Remove paper backing from buckram appliqués and fuse together. Remove paper backing from organza appliqués and fuse one to each side of buckram appliqués.
18. Glue 16-gauge wire to top back of wings along edges. Glue cording along front and back edges of wings.
19. To hang wings, punch two small holes in wings where indicated on pattern. Cut two 3" lengths of 16-gauge wire; thread one wire through each hole and around a back rib on small frame. Twist wires together to secure.
20. Paint star red, then *Sponge Paint*, page 184, gold. Use sequin pins to add 4mm and 8mm round beads to star. Poke two holes in back of star, then thread 20-gauge wire through holes and around arms; twist wire around itself to secure.

Christmas is for Children

CRAFT FOAM ORNAMENTS

(shown on pages 14 and 16)

You will need tracing paper; blue, red, yellow, green, and white craft foam; craft knife and cutting mat; fabric glue; S-Hook Hangers (this page); double-sided tape; plastic-coated twist ties; and a ¼" dia. and ⅛" dia. hole punch.

Allow glue to dry after each application.

Spiral

1. Trace the spiral pattern, page 165, onto tracing paper; cut out. Use pattern to cut two spirals from one color of foam.
2. Glue straight ends of shapes together to make a whole ornament. Hang from tree.

Top

1. Trace the heart pattern, page 165, onto tracing paper; cut out. Use pattern to cut one heart each from yellow, white, green, blue, and red foam.
2. Use the craft knife to score down the center of each heart.
3. Fold each heart in half, then taping the hearts together as you go, stack the hearts on top of each other. Apply several pieces of tape across the folded edges of the heart stack.
4. Bend twist tie in half forming a loop, then adhere each end to the tape on edges of stack.
5. Fan out ornament and tape together to secure. Hang with an S-Hook Hanger.

Snowflake

1. Trace the snowflake pattern, page 165, onto tracing paper; cut out. Use pattern to cut two snowflakes from foam.
2. Punch ¼" dia. and ⅛" dia. holes in each piece as indicated on pattern.
3. Slide the pieces together.
4. Punch a ¼" dia. hole in the top of the snowflake. Hang with an S-Hook Hanger.

Santa Hat

1. Trace hat, trim, and pom-pom patterns, page 165, onto tracing paper; cut out. Use patterns to cut hat from red foam and trim and two pom-poms from white foam.
2. Overlapping slightly, glue hat piece together along straight edges.
3. Matching ends at seam of hat, glue trim along bottom edge of hat.
4. Catching tip of hat and S-Hook Hanger between them, glue pom-poms together.

S-HOOK HANGER

(shown on page 16)

Trace S-hook hanger pattern, page 165, onto tracing paper; cut out. Use pattern to cut hanger from craft foam.

CRAFT FOAM GARLAND

(shown on page 16)

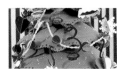

You will need yellow, blue, red, and green craft foam; fabric glue; craft knife and cutting mat; and double-sided tape.

1. For rope, twist two ⅛" x 18" strips of yellow foam together; glue ends and spot glue twists along rope to secure.
2. For each ball, cut one yellow, one blue, two red, and two green 1⅛" dia. circles from foam. Follow Steps 2 and 3 of the Top Ornament (this page) to attach circles together.
3. Spacing evenly and using tape to secure, fan out ball around rope.
4. To hang garland, insert ends of garland through holes in tree.

WHIMSICAL FOAM STOCKING

(shown on page 17)

You will need red, green, yellow, blue, and white craft foam; tracing paper; scalloped-edge craft scissors; The Ultimate! glue by Crafter's Pick™; white and yellow self-adhesive foam boarders; hole punch; yellow, red, and blue chenille stems; and ribbon.

1. Enlarge stocking pattern, page 175, and band pattern, page 166, 170%; cut out. Using patterns, cut two stocking shapes from red foam and one band from green foam.
2. Trace greenery pattern, page 168, onto tracing paper; cut out. Using pattern and craft scissors, cut three greenery pieces from green foam.
3. Cut fifteen 1¾" dia. circles out of desired foam colors.
4. Leaving top open, glue stocking shapes together along edges. Glue band along top of stocking. Adhere borders to band.

5. For dots, punch several holes in scrap pieces of each color of foam. Glue seven circles to stocking, then glue dots to circles and along borders.

6. Punch holes along edges of greenery pieces. Glue the straight edge of one piece along the back of the stocking, then gather and glue remaining pieces to chenille stems.

7. For circle flowers, glue dots to remaining circles, then glue each flower to a chenille stem.

8. Follow Steps 1 – 3 of Top Ornaments, page 124, to make three "top" flowers. Center chenille stem on folded edge of stack, then make two loops in chenille stem at top of flower; glue to secure.

9. Curl, then glue chenille stems inside stocking.

10. For hanger, glue a loop of ribbon to back of stocking.

CRAFT FOAM CHRISTMAS TREE

(shown on page 16)

You will need 1" and ³/₈" dia. dowels; sandpaper; spray primer; 12" square wooden plaque for base; four 1¹/₂"w wooden wheels for feet; green and red spray paint; four 1"-long wood screws; drill and drill bits; hot glue gun; one brown, eleven green, and one yellow 3mm-thick 12" x 18" craft foam sheets; tracing paper; deckled-edge and scalloped-edge craft scissors; drawing compass; hole punch; ⁵/₈"w green grosgrain ribbon; and pinking shears.

Use scalloped-edge craft scissors to cut out all tiers of tree from green foam. Refer to tree diagram when assembling tier layers.

1. For base of tree, cut a 30" length of 1" dia. dowel and a 4" length of ³/₈" dia. dowel.

2. Sand, then prime, all wooden pieces. Paint dowels green and base and wheels red.

3. Using wood screws, attach one foot at each corner on the bottom of the base.

4. Drill a pilot hole through the center of the base and one end of the 1" dia. dowel (bottom of trunk). Drill a ³/₈" dia. hole, 1¹/₄" deep in remaining end of dowel (top of trunk).

5. Use one screw to attach bottom of trunk to base; add remaining screws around center screw to secure.

6. Cover bottom 11" of trunk with brown foam.

7. For bark, use deckled-edge scissors to cut strips of brown foam to layer and glue on trunk.

8. Trace tree top pattern, page 168, onto tracing paper; cut out. Cut tree top from green foam.

9. Following *Making a Whole Pattern*, page 184, and using the half tier pattern, page 167, make a whole pattern. Use whole pattern to cut three A tiers.

10. For tiers B and C, enlarge whole pattern 125% and 145%. Use enlarged patterns to cut out one B tier and two C tiers.

11. Enlarge the half tier pattern on page 167, 175% and 200%; cut out (do not make into whole patterns).

12. For two-piece tiers D and E, use the 175% pattern to cut out two D tiers and the 200% pattern to cut out four E tiers.

13. For each two-piece tier, overlap and glue one straight edge of two pieces together.

14. Using compass, draw a ³/₄" dia. half-circle at center of each tier along straight edge; cut out and clip along curves. Punch holes along outer edge of each tier.

15. Referring to Fig. 1, mark dowel for tier placement.

Fig. 1

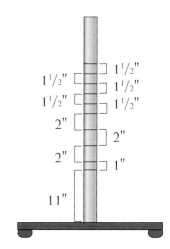

16. Starting with bottom tier (E) and referring to Fig. 2, glue tier around pole. Glue a length of ribbon over clipped edge of tier, then glue a strip of foam to underside of tier and onto trunk for added support. Carefully bend down tier; shape and glue edges together. Repeat for remaining tiers.

Fig. 2

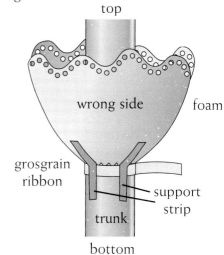

17. For tree top, use hot glue to secure ³/₈" dia. dowel in top of trunk. Wrap tree top around dowel and glue edges together.

18. Trace star patterns, page 167, onto tracing paper; cut out. Using patterns and pinking shears, cut out two of the largest star shapes from yellow foam, then using regular scissors, cut two of each remaining star shape from yellow foam.

19. Stack and glue each set of stars together from largest to smallest. Matching sets, glue stars together around dowel.

Tree Diagram

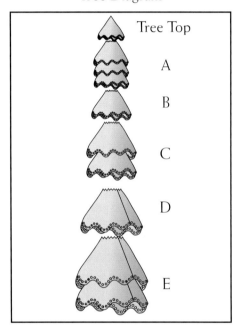

COUNTDOWN SANTA
(shown on page 17)

You will need tracing paper; transfer paper and stylus; flesh-colored, white, and red craft foam sheets; pink, blue, and white acrylic paint and paintbrushes; The Ultimate! glue by Crafter's Pick™; assorted colors of pre-cut craft foam self-adhesive numbers; double-sided self-adhesive foam sheets cut into ¼"w strips; fabric glue; gold 18-gauge craft wire; and ¼"w ribbon.

Use The Ultimate! glue for all gluing unless otherwise indicated; allow all glue to dry after each application.

1. (*Note:* Cut three beard sections and do not cut beard accent pieces.) Enlarge Santa patterns, page 170, 125% and follow *Stacked or Overlapped Patterns*, page 184, to make each pattern piece. Using patterns and referring to color key, cut pieces from foam.

2. Trace pocket pattern, page 166, onto tracing paper; cut out. Use pattern to cut 24 pockets from white foam.

3. Position pieces on face and mark cheek placement; remove pieces, then paint cheeks pink.

4. Glue beard sections together with the second section extending 5½" from lowest point of first section and third section extending 4½" from the lowest point of the second section; glue beard to face.

5. Arrange and glue cutouts on face, hat, and beard.

6. For each eye, paint a blue center with a white hightlight. Glue eyes in place.

7. Attach numbers to pockets. Cutting adhesive strips to fit, position, then adhere pockets to beard. For added security, add a drop of fabric glue at each corner of the pockets.

8. Form wire into eye glasses, then insert wire ends into foam next to eyes; bend ends and glue at back to secure.

9. For hanger, glue a loop of ribbon to the back of Santa's head.

SANTA'S TRAIN
(shown on pages 14, 15, and 17)

You will need a saw; ½"-thick plywood; four wooden crates (ours measure 9½" x 12½" x 18"); ¾"-, 1"-, and 2"-long wood screws; ¾" metal pipe clamps; four 1" dia. x 1½"-long eyehooks; ¾" dia. wooden dowels;

drill and bits; sandpaper; twelve 1"-thick x 5" dia. wooden plaques; tack cloth; blue, yellow, white, and red acrylic paint; paintbrushes; The Ultimate! glue by Crafter's Pick™; blue, yellow, red, green, white, black, and flesh-colored 2mm-thick large craft foam sheets; fabric glue; decorative-edge craft scissors; twelve ¾" dia. nuts; hole punch; tracing paper; nylon rope; four heavy-duty snap hooks; cardboard; pinking shears; pink, blue, and white acrylic paint and paintbrushes.

Use The Ultimate! glue for all gluing unless otherwise indicated; allow glue to dry after each application.

Boxcars

1. For each boxcar, cut a piece of plywood the same size as bottom of crate; trim each long edge ½". Use 1" screws to attach plywood to bottom of crate along front and back edges. Referring to Fig. 1, use ¾" screws to attach pipe clamps to bottom of crate, then attach eyehooks.

Fig. 1

2. For wheel axles, measure across crate and add 1". Cut two axles from dowels the determined measurement, then drill a pilot hole in the center of each end of each axle. Sand the crate, axles, and four plaques, then wipe with tack cloth. Paint the crate the desired color and the axles and plaques white.

3. Aligning straight edge of foam to top edge of crate, glue foam to sides of crate; trim bottom edge as necessary. Use craft scissors to trim ends of foam pieces for front and back of crate; wrapping ends to sides of crate, glue trimmed foam to crate; cut away foam covering the handles.

4. For each wheel, drill a pilot hole through the center of one of the plaques. Center and glue a nut around the hole on the back of each plaque. Use a screw to attach one wheel to one end of each axle. Slide axles through clamps on bottom of car, then attach remaining wheels. Cut a 5" dia. circle from one color of foam and a 2" dia. circle from another color of foam; punch five dots from a third color of foam. Glue the large circle to the wheel; center and glue the small circle to the large circle. Glue the dots to the small circle.

5. For the "light cords," cut $^1/8$"w strips of green foam. Piecing as necessary, twist the strips together and use fabric glue to adhere along the side of the car. Trace the bulb and socket patterns from page 167 onto tracing paper; cut out.

6. For each light, use the patterns to cut one socket from green foam and one each top, middle, and bottom bulb from desired color of foam. Stacking bulb pieces from largest to smallest, glue bulbs $^1/4$" below cord…placing a bulb below a pieced section of cord will conceal the overlap when the socket is added. Glue sockets to lights, "connecting" them to cord.

7. Tie each end of a length of rope to snap hooks…these will snap onto the eyehooks to connect the cars.

Engine

1. Follow Step 1 of Boxcars to prepare base of engine.

2. Cut a piece of plywood the same size at top of crate. Use 2" screws to attach plywood piece to top of engine.

3. Follow Step 2 of Boxcars to prepare axles, engine, wheels, and remaining crate. Paint axles and wheels white and engine and crate red.

4. Use 1" screws to attach red crate to engine for cab.

5. Enlarge cowcatcher and cowcatcher inset patterns, page 166, 105%. Follow *Making a Whole Pattern*, page 184, to make a whole cowcatcher pattern.

6. Trace the smoke stack cap and triangle patterns, pages 168 and 169, onto tracing paper.

7. Using the patterns, cut cap and two large and two small cowcatcher insets from black foam. Cut one cowcatcher from blue foam and one cowcatcher and one triangle from cardboard. Cut one 3" x 13$^1/2$" piece of black foam for smoke stack.

8. Aligning bottom edges, glue triangle to center front of engine. Glue foam cowcatcher to cardboard cowcatcher. Score cowcatcher down center on cardboard side, bend gently and glue to engine along edges of triangle; glue insets to cowcatcher.

9. Overlap and glue ends of smoke stack together; glue to top of engine. Glue ends of cap together, then glue to top of smoke stack.

10. For each headlight, use pinking shears to cut one 3" dia. base from blue foam and one 2$^1/4$" dia. top, one 2$^1/2$" dia. middle, and one 2$^3/4$" dia. bottom light from desired color of foam. Stack and glue light pieces to base.

11. Mitering corners, glue 1"w strips of yellow foam to side of cab for window.

12. Enlarge Santa and arm patterns, pages 170 and 171, 125% and follow *Stacked or Overlapped Patterns*, page 184, to make each pattern piece. Using patterns and referring to color key, cut pieces from foam. Referring to the photo, page 17, paint cheeks pink, then arrange and glue Santa onto side of cab. For eyes, paint a blue center and a white highlight.

13. Knot a length of rope to a piece of dowel; poke dowel and knot through handle hole in front of engine. Knot remaining end of rope.

A Splendid Evening

BEADED CANDLESCAPE

(shown on page 20)

You will need a 17½" square piece of purple silk fabric, beading thread and needle, 4mm silver beads and other assorted silver, purple, and clear beads, 11" square silver footed tray, assorted size purple candles, artificial Ming fern, Snowflake Candle Pins (page 131), and glass gems.

1. For the fabric square, hem fabric piece ½" on each edge.
2. For each beaded dangle, make a knot in one end of a length of thread, then run the thread through the fabric. Add desired beads; run thread around last bead and back up through dangle and fabric, then knot thread to secure. Spacing dangles evenly, add dangles along the edges of fabric square (Fig. 1).

Fig. 1

3. Spacing evenly, sew 4mm silver beads to fabric piece along hemline.
4. Place tray on fabric square. Arrange candles and fern on tray; add Snowflake Candle Pins to candles and beads and gems to arrangement as desired.

PILLOW ORNAMENTS

(shown on page 21)

You will need assorted light purple fabrics, disappearing ink fabric-marking pen, beading needle and thread, 6mm dark purple and 1.5mm light purple bugle beads, assorted light and dark purple seed beads, 6mm clear cone beads, clear leaf beads, clear heart beads, 14mm clear flower slide bead and 12mm clear flat beads for centers, 8mm clear flower beads, ⅛" dia. light purple cording, and tracing paper.

Note: For long rows of beads, thread several beads onto needle, then go down into fabric and bring needle back up through last bead; repeat as needed to secure line of beads. Follow project instructions for ending row.

Small Snowflake

1. Cut two 4" squares from fabric.
2. Find center of one square, then use pen to draw an eight point starburst with alternating 1"- and 1¼"-long spokes onto right side of square (draw one 1¼" spoke pointing toward each corner).
3. For each long spoke, work from the center out and thread one 6mm bugle, twelve seed, one cone, one leaf, then one seed bead onto needle; go back down through leaf and fabric, then secure line of beads.

4. For each short spoke, work from the center out and thread one 6mm bugle, seven seed, one cone, one leaf, then one seed bead onto needle; go back down through leaf and fabric, then secure line of beads.
5. Attach one heart bead between each spoke.
6. For snowflake center, attach 14mm clear flower slide bead.
7. For hanger, fold a 5" length of cording in half, then match ends of hanger to center edge on right side of one square and tack in place.
8. Matching right sides, leaving an opening for turning, and using a ½" seam allowance, sew squares together. Clip corners, then turn ornament right side out; sew opening closed.

Large Snowflake

1. Cut two 5" squares from fabric.
2. Find center of one square, then use pen to draw a six-point starburst with 1¼"-long spokes onto right side of square.
3. For each spoke, work from the center out and thread twenty 1.5mm bugle, one 8mm flower, then one seed bead onto needle; go back down through flower and fabric, then secure line of beads. Halfway down spoke, thread two 1.5mm bugle, one leaf, then one seed bead onto needle; go down through fabric and secure; repeat on remaining side of spoke.

4. Between each spoke, thread one 1.5mm bugle, one heart, then two seed beads onto needle; go down through fabric and secure.

5. For snowflake center, thread a 12mm clear flat bead then a purple seed bead onto needle; go back down through large bead and fabric and secure.

6. For hanger, fold a 5" length of cording in half, then match ends of hanger to center edge on right side of one square and tack in place.

7. Matching right sides, leaving an opening for turning, and using a $1/2$" seam allowance, sew squares together. Clip corners, then turn ornament right side out; sew opening closed.

Eight-Point Star

1. Cut two 4" squares from fabric.
2. Find center of one square, then use pen to draw an eight point starburst with alternating 1"- and $1^1/8$"-long spokes onto right side of square (draw one $1^1/8$" spoke pointing toward each corner).
3. For each long spoke, work from the center out and thread twelve dark purple seed, one 6mm bugle, then three dark purple seed beads onto needle; go back down through last seed bead and fabric, then secure line of beads.
4. For each short spoke, work from the center out and thread eight dark purple seed, one 6mm bugle, then three dark purple seed beads onto needle; go back down through last seed bead and fabric, then secure line of beads.

5. Bead around each spoke with 1.5mm bugle beads.
6. For star center, thread a 12mm clear flat bead then a purple seed bead onto needle; go back down through large bead and fabric and secure.
7. For hanger, fold a 5" length of cording in half, then match ends of hanger to center edge on right side of one square and tack in place.
8. Matching right sides, leaving an opening for turning, and using a $1/2$" seam allowance, sew squares together. Clip corners, then turn ornament right side out; sew opening closed.

Four-Point Star

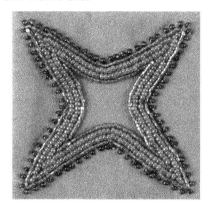

1. Cut two 4" squares from fabric.
2. Trace four-point star pattern, page 171, onto tracing paper; cut out just inside drawn lines. Draw around pattern on center right side of one square.
3. Attach a row of 1.5mm bugle beads along pattern lines. Attach two rows of light purple seed beads outside the first row, then another row of 1.5mm bugle beads.
4. Attach a row of evenly spaced dark purple seed beads just outside star.
5. For hanger, fold a 5" length of cording in half, then match ends of hanger to center edge on right side of one square and tack in place.
6. Matching right sides, leaving an opening for turning, and using a $1/2$" seam allowance, sew squares together. Clip corners, then turn ornament right side out; sew opening closed.

Circle

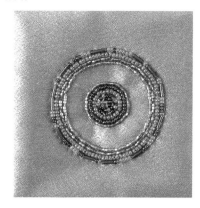

1. Cut two 4" squares from fabric.
2. Use pen to draw a $7/8$" dia. circle and a $1^3/4$" dia. circle at center on right side of one square.
3. For inner circle, attach a row of 1.5mm bugle beads along center drawn line. Working toward the center, attach a row of dark purple seed beads, then a row of light purple seed beads; fill in center of circle with beads as desired.
4. For outer circle, attach a row of 1.5mm bugle beads along outer drawn line. Repeat to attach another row of 1.5mm bugle beads outside the first row, then a row of light purple seed beads. Alternating the seed beads and the 6mm bugle beads, attach the last row of beads.
5. For hanger, fold a 5" length of cording in half, then match ends of hanger to center edge on right side of one square and tack in place.
6. Matching right sides, leaving an opening for turning, and using a $1/2$" seam allowance, sew squares together. Clip corners, then turn ornament right side out; sew opening closed.

BEADED WIRE ORNAMENTS
(shown on pages 19 and 21)

You will need wire cutters; Memory Wire® for bracelets; needle-nose pliers; assorted sizes and styles of silver, clear, light blue, and light purple beads; ⁵/₈"w light purple sheer ribbon; and tinsel thread.

Wreath

1. Cut a length of wire that coils three times.
2. Bend one end of wire into a loop to prevent beads from slipping off; thread beads onto wire, then bend remaining end of wire into a loop.
3. For hanger, thread a 13" length each of ribbon and tinsel thread through wreath and knot ends together.

Icicle

1. Cut three, one-coil lengths of wire.
2. For each ring, bend one end of one wire ring into a loop to prevent beads from slipping off; thread beads onto wire. Thread remaining end of wire through first loop, then bend it into a loop to secure.
3. Repeat Step 2 for each additional ring, slipping next ring through previous ring before securing.
4. Knot short lengths of tinsel thread in several places on each ring.

BEADED BOWS
(shown on page 21)

For each bow, you will need 1¹/₂"w light purple wire-edged ribbon, chenille stem or craft wire, hot glue gun, 1"-long beaded trim, beading needle and thread, 4mm silver beads and 6mm light purple miracle beads, paintbrush, light purple acrylic paint, and a 1³/₄"-long wooden clothespin.

1. For each bow, use a 26" length of ribbon and follow *Making a Simple Bow*, page 152, to make a bow with 6"-long streamers and two 6" loops.
2. For center loop, press edges and one end of a 2³/₄" length of ribbon ¹/₄" to wrong side. Wrapping ends to center back, glue a length of trim along pressed end of ribbon. Wrap loop piece around center of bow; glue in place.
3. Wrapping ends to back, glue a length of trim along end of each streamer.
4. For additional beading along each length of trim, sew alternating silver and purple beads along flange of trim.
5. Paint clothespin and allow to dry, then glue it to back of bow. Use clothespin to attach bow to tree.

LAVENDER CENTERPIECE
(shown on page 22)

You will need 1¹/₂"w light purple satin and 2"w light purple sheer ribbon; tinsel thread; 23" dia. clear and frosted petal acrylic wreath; hot glue gun; 2¹/₄" dia. silver, 2¹/₄" dia. pearl, and 2¹/₂" dia. light purple glass ornaments; artificial Ming fern; six Beaded Wire Wreath Ornaments without hangers (this page); 13" dia. silver charger; assorted candles; and assorted beads.

1. Wind ribbons and tinsel thread through wreath.
2. Spacing evenly, glue a silver, pearl, and light purple ornament cluster in three places on the wreath.
3. Tuck and glue greenery throughout the wreath until desired coverage is achieved.
4. Place Beaded Wire Wreath Ornaments on wreath as desired.
5. Place wreath on charger, then arrange candles in the center.
6. Sprinkle beads on charger and glue several beads to wreath as desired.

SNOWFLAKE CANDLE PINS

(shown on pages 22 and 23)

For each pin, thread one seed bead, one miracle bead, then one ³/₄"w silver snowflake charm onto a silver sequin pin. Insert pin into a candle to decorate.

BEADED SPREADER

(shown on page 22)

You will need wire cutters and needle-nose pliers; 20- and 32-gauge wire; small silver cheese spreader with looped handle (ours measures 6"-long); light blue, light purple, and purple seed beads; 6mm and 4mm light purple miracle beads; flat light blue oval beads; and 8mm silver beads.

1. Cut a length of 20-gauge wire four times the length of the spreader handle.
2. Bend one end of wire into a loop to prevent beads from slipping off, then add one blue seed and one 6mm miracle bead; thread wire through loop in end of spreader, then wrap handle with wire, adding two oval beads evenly spaced along handle. To finish off wire at base of blade, add one silver, one 4mm miracle, one blue seed, one 6mm miracle, one blue seed, and one 4mm miracle bead, then loop end to prevent beads from slipping off.
3. Bend one end of a length of 32-gauge wire into a loop to prevent beads from slipping off. Thread wire with one blue seed, one 4mm miracle, one silver, then alternate between light purple and purple seed beads until a length is achieved to wrap handle.

1. Wrap handle with beaded wire, then twist wire around 20-gauge wire to secure.

LAVENDER TABLE RUNNER

(shown on page 23)

You will need four coordinating shades of light purple fabrics; disappearing ink fabric-marking pen; beading needle and thread; 1.5mm light purple and 6mm dark purple bugle beads, dark purple and light purple seed beads, 4mm silver beads, and 6mm light purple miracle beads; fabric glue; and two 14¹/₂" pieces of 1"-long beaded trim with satin flange.

Use a ¹/₂" seam allowance for all sewing.

1. Cut one 14¹/₂" x 16" piece for A panel, two 14¹/₂" x 16" pieces for B panels, two 9" x 14¹/₂" pieces for C panels, and one 14¹/₂" x 54" piece for backing from coordinating fabrics.
2. Referring to Fig. 1 for runner front and matching right sides and 14¹/₂" edges, sew one B panel to each end of A panel.

Fig. 1

3. Matching right sides, sew one C panel to each end of B panels.
4. Follow Steps 2 – 4 of the Circle Pillow Ornament, page 129, to add several beaded circles to each C panel.

5. Alternating 4mm silver and miracle beads and leaving the seam allowance unbeaded, tack a looping strand of beads along the seam of each C panel.
6. Matching right sides and leaving an opening for turning, sew runner front and back together. Clip corners and turn right side out; sew opening closed.
7. Wrapping ends to back, glue beaded trim along ends of runner.
8. Spacing bead sets evenly along flange of trim and being careful not to work through backing, sew sets of one light purple seed bead, one 4mm silver bead, then one light purple seed bead along each flange.

STAINED GLASS PLATES

(shown on page 24)

For each plate, you will need clear self-adhesive vinyl, clear glass plate, and spray paint for glass.

1. Cut small square and rectangular shapes from vinyl; cut smaller shapes inside larger shapes. Adhere shapes to back rim of plate as desired.
2. Follow manufacturer's instructions to apply paint to back of plate.
3. Once dry, carefully remove vinyl pieces.

Tip To prevent marring the painted surface when removing vinyl cutouts, use the tip of a craft knife to lift up the corner of each piece, then carefully peel them off.

BEADED COCKTAIL SETS

(shown on page 24)

For each set, you will need clear self-adhesive vinyl; spray paint for glass; champagne flute; 24-gauge wire; wire cutters and needle-nose pliers; assorted beads; two $^3/_4$"w snowflake charms; hot glue gun; beading needle and thread; and a linen cocktail napkin.

Champagne Flute

1. Follow Steps 1 – 3 of the Stained Glass Plates (page 131) to paint bottom of flute.
2. Bend one end of a 7$^3/_4$" length of wire into a loop to prevent beads from slipping off, then thread wire with assorted beads. Form a loop in remaining end of wire; add snowflake charm, then glue a bead to the center of the snowflake.
3. Wrap wire around stem of glass.

Cocktail Napkin

1. Follow Step 2 of Beaded Candlescape, page 128, to make and sew a beaded dangle to each corner of the napkin.
2. Sew a charm, with a bead at its center, to one corner of the napkin.

Tip Matching the beads on the snowflakes for each Beaded Cocktail set will make it easier to distinguish everyone's drinks.

LAVENDER TREE TOPPER

(shown on page 24)

Wire several pieces of artificial Ming fern together to form a swag, then with garland extending above and below swag, wire several lengths of sparkle twig garland to center of swag. Cover center of arrangement by wiring on a cluster of silver, light purple, and pearl glass ornaments.

BLUSHING CHAMPAGNE PUNCH

(shown on page 24)

1 bottle (32 ounces) cranberry-grape juice cocktail, chilled
1 bottle (32 ounces) unsweetened apple juice, chilled
1 bottle (750 milliliters) champagne, chilled

Combine cranberry-grape juice cocktail and apple juice in a large punch bowl; stir well. Add champagne just before serving.
Yield: 2$^3/_4$ quarts punch

CHEESE SOUFFLÉ SANDWICHES

(shown on page 23)

3 loaves (16 ounces each) sandwich bread (see Note)
1 pound butter or margarine, softened
4 jars (5 ounces each) sharp process cheese spread, softened
1 teaspoon onion powder
1$^1/_2$ teaspoons Worcestershire sauce
1 teaspoon hot sauce
1 teaspoon Beau Monde seasoning
1$^1/_2$ teaspoons minced fresh dill (see Note)

Remove crusts from bread; reserve for other uses. Beat butter and cheese spread at medium speed with an electric mixer until light and fluffy. Add onion powder and next 4 ingredients. Spread cheese mixture over 3 slices of bread. Stack slices; cut stack into 4 pieces. Spread sides with cheese mixture. Repeat procedure with remaining bread slices and cheese mixture. (Sandwiches may be frozen at this stage, and thawed before baking.) Bake at 325° for 10 to 15 minutes or until edges are golden.
Yield: 6 dozen sandwiches
Note: Slices don't crumble as easily if bread is chilled before being spread with cheese mixture. For variety, try olive and pimento cheese spread instead of sharp, and substitute chives for the dill; garnish with pimiento-stuffed olive slices.

PHYLLO SUSHI ROLLS

(shown on page 23)

- 2 cups water
- 1 cup uncooked short-grain rice
- 2 tablespoons seasoned rice vinegar
- 1 tablespoon sugar
- 1 teaspoon salt
- 1 jar (6 ounces) pickled ginger
- 1/4 cup fresh lime juice
- 1 1/2 tablespoons dark sesame oil
- 2 tablespoons soy sauce
- 1 tuna steak (8 ounces and about 5 inches long)
- 8 sheets frozen phyllo pastry, thawed
  Vegetable cooking spray
- 8 sheets nori, cut into 7 x 6-inch rectangles (see Note)
  Wasabi (see Note)

Bring water to a boil; stir in rice. Cover; reduce heat, and simmer 20 minutes or until liquid is absorbed and rice is tender. Stir in vinegar, sugar, and salt. Cover and chill thoroughly.

Drain pickled ginger, reserving 1/4 cup juice. Combine reserved ginger juice and next 3 ingredients; stir well. Cut tuna lengthwise into 8 strips; place strips in a heavy-duty, zip-top plastic bag. Pour half the juice mixture over tuna. Seal bag. Chill 30 minutes.

Unfold phyllo; cover with plastic wrap and a damp towel to prevent drying. Fold 1 sheet of phyllo crosswise in half; spray pastry with cooking spray. Place 1 nori sheet on bottom edge of pastry. Spoon 3 tablespoons rice mixture across 1 short end of nori. Place 1 strip of tuna on rice mixture. Spoon 3 tablespoons rice mixture over tuna.

Roll up, tucking in pastry edges as you roll. Place on a baking sheet lined with parchment paper. Repeat procedure with remaining phyllo, nori, rice mixture, and tuna.

Bake at 450° for 10 minutes or until golden. Cut each roll in half diagonally. Serve with remaining juice mixture, pickled ginger, and wasabi.

Yield: 16 appetizer servings

Note: Nori is a paper-thin sheet of dried seaweed that is generally used for wrapping sushi and rice balls. Wasabi is a pungent vegetable which is grated and used as a condiment with sushi. It can be purchased as a paste or as a powder. Since it has a very spicy hot flavor, many times it is mixed with soy sauce. These items can be found in Japanese markets and some supermarkets.

CHICKEN SATÉ WITH PEANUT SAUCE

(shown on page 23)

- 2 teaspoons minced fresh ginger
- 4 garlic cloves, quartered
- 1 cup loosely packed fresh cilantro leaves
- 2 tablespoons honey
- 1/2 cup creamy peanut butter
- 1/3 cup lite soy sauce
- 1 1/2 tablespoons fresh lemon juice
- 2 tablespoons dark sesame oil
- 1/2 teaspoon crushed red pepper
- 2 tablespoons water
- 4 to 5 pounds uncooked chicken tenders or boneless chicken breasts, cut into pieces

Combine ginger and next 9 ingredients in a food processor. Process until well blended, stopping to scrape down sides.

Thread 1 piece of chicken onto each of twenty-four 6-inch skewers. Measure 1/4 cup peanut sauce and brush on chicken. Reserve remaining sauce. Broil 3 minutes on each side or until done. Serve with reserved sauce.

Yield: 24 appetizer servings

BOILED SHRIMP WITH ZIPPY COCKTAIL SAUCE

(shown on page 23)

Simplify your food preparation by buying boiled shrimp from the seafood market.

- 1 cup chili sauce
- 1 cup ketchup
- 2 tablespoons prepared horseradish
- 2 tablespoons picante sauce or salsa
- 3 tablespoons lemon juice
- 2 tablespoons Worcestershire sauce
- 1 teaspoon onion powder
- 1 teaspoon garlic powder
- 3 pounds unpeeled large shrimp, boiled

Combine all ingredients except shrimp, stirring well. Cover and chill at least 2 hours. Serve with boiled shrimp.

Yield: 2 1/3 cups sauce

CURRIED CHUTNEY SPREAD

(shown on page 23)

2 packages (8 ounces each) cream
    cheese, softened
$^{1}/_{2}$ cup chutney
$1^{1}/_{2}$ teaspoons curry powder
$^{3}/_{4}$ cup finely chopped pecans
$^{1}/_{4}$ cup chopped sweetened dried
    cranberries
$^{1}/_{4}$ cup chopped dried apricots

Combine first 3 ingredients in a
mixing bowl; beat at medium speed of
an electric mixer until blended. Stir in
pecans, cranberries, and apricots.
Spoon mixture into a serving bowl;
cover and chill at least 8 hours.
Serve with apple slices, celery sticks,
gingersnaps, or crackers.
Yield: $3^{1}/_{3}$ cups spread

CHOCOLATE-RASPBERRY TRUFFLES

(shown on page 25)

*These chocolate delights are perfect for a special
holiday occasion.*

$1^{1}/_{3}$ cups (8 ounces) semisweet
    chocolate morsels
2 tablespoons whipping cream
1 tablespoon butter
2 tablespoons seedless raspberry
    jam
6 ounces milk chocolate or white
    chocolate
2 teaspoons shortening

Combine chocolate morsels, cream,
and butter in a double boiler; bring
water to a boil. Reduce heat to low;
cook, stirring constantly, until
chocolate morsels melt; stir in jam.
Remove from heat; cover and freeze
mixture 30 minutes or until firm.

Shape mixture into 1-inch balls.
Place on wax paper-lined baking
sheets; chill 5 minutes. If necessary,
reroll to smooth balls. Freeze 8 hours.

Place chocolate and shortening in
top of a double boiler; bring water to a
boil. Reduce heat to low; cook, stirring
constantly, until chocolate and
shortening melt. Place each ball on a
candy dipper or fork, and hold over
double boiler. Quickly spoon melted
chocolate mixture over each ball,
allowing excess to drip back into
double boiler. Return each ball to lined
baking sheets. Drizzle additional
chocolate with a fork over balls for a
decorative touch; chill until firm. Store
in an airtight container in refrigerator.
Yield: $2^{1}/_{2}$ dozen truffles

EASY PETITS FOURS

(shown on page 25)

2 loaves (10.75 ounces each)
    pound cake
8 squares (2 ounces each) vanilla-
    flavored almond bark candy
    coating
$^{1}/_{2}$ cup whipping cream
1 tube (0.68 ounce) purple
    decorating gel
    Silver dragées (see Note)

Trim $^{1}/_{4}$ inch off top and sides of
each cake. Cut each cake into five
$1^{1}/_{2}$-inch-thick slices; cut each slice
into two $1^{1}/_{2}$-inch-thick squares. Place
squares on a cooling rack over a
jellyroll pan.

Combine candy coating and
whipping cream in a double boiler;
bring to a boil. Reduce heat to low;
cook, stirring constantly, until candy
coating melts. Spoon coating over cake
squares, covering top and sides. When
all the coating has been used from the
double boiler, scrape the coating from
the jellyroll pan into the double boiler
and remelt. Continue spooning over
cake squares until coated. Allow
coating to set up.

Using decorating gel, pipe desired
designs on top of petits fours. Place
silver dragées on cakes, as desired.
Yield: 20 petits fours
Note: Silver dragées are nonedible and
recommended for decoration only.

Updated Classics

TREE PLANTER

(shown on page 26)

You will need burnt umber spray primer for metal, metal ceiling tiles, burnt umber and ivory acrylic paint, paintbrushes, wooden or resin planter box to fit tree, sandpaper, tack cloth, and craft glue.

1. Prime tiles.
2. Paint planter and tiles burnt umber, then paint them ivory.
3. To create an aged look, lightly sand planter and tiles revealing some of the base coat; wipe with tack cloth.
4. Glue tiles to sides of planter.

COVERED STOOL

(shown on page 27)

You will need a wooden bar stool, 2"-thick foam, high-loft batting, fabric, heavy-duty staple gun, hot glue gun, and 3 1/2"-long tassel fringe.

1. Draw around stool seat on wrong side of foam, two layers of batting, and fabric; cut out foam along drawn line, batting just inside drawn line, and fabric 6" outside drawn line.

Tip Textured wallpaper can be used in place of the ceiling tiles to decorate the planter.

2. Center and layer batting, foam, then stool seat on wrong side of fabric piece.
3. Pulling fabric taut, staple center of opposite edges of fabric to bottom of seat.
4. Clipping and folding fabric at legs to ease in place, and smoothing fabric evenly around seat, continue stapling edges in place as you go.
5. Trim excess fabric from bottom of seat as necessary.
6. Glue a length of fringe along edge of seat.

CINCHED VALANCE

(shown on page 26)

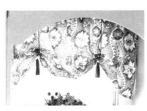

You will need fabric, 3/4" dia. tension rod to fit window, and two corded tassels.

1. Measure inside width of window; add 1". Measure from inside top of window to desired length for valance; add 17". Cut a piece of fabric the determined measurements.
2. For fabric panel, make a 1/2" hem along sides and bottom of fabric piece.
3. For rod casing, press top edge of panel 1/2" to wrong side; press panel 2 1/2" to wrong side again. Topstitch casing along bottom fold and 1 1/2" below top fold.
4. Adjust rod to fit window, then place panel on rod and hang it in window.
5. With each tassel at bottom of fabric and one cord on each side of fabric, gather fabric and tie cords together at top of shade.
6. Evenly space cords on shade.

BERRIED WREATH AND TREETOP WREATH

(shown on pages 26 and 30)

For the wreaths, you will need a hot glue gun, one 8" dia. and one 14" dia. grapevine wreath, 2 3/8" red and cream wire-edged ribbon, red raspberry and boxwood picks, and a strand of white lights for the treetop wreath.

Gluing ends to secure, wrap each wreath with ribbon. Arrange and glue picks of raspberry and boxwood to wreaths until desired fullness is achieved.

For the treetop wreath, wrap the 8" wreath with lights, then connect lights to tree lights.

NIGHTLIGHT

(shown on page 31)

You will need a self-adhesive nightlight kit, fabric, hot glue gun, cording, and a tassel tie.

1. Follow the manufacturer's instructions to cover nightlight shade with fabric.
2. Beginning and ending at top center, glue cording along edges of shade.
3. Tie tassel into a bow and glue it to shade.

CROSS-STITCHED SANTAS

(shown on pages 28 and 30)

Cross-Stitched Afghan

Refer to Cross Stitch, page 185, while working project. Follow the chart and stitch key, page 171. Use three strands of floss for Cross Stitch and one strand for Half Cross Stitch, Backstitch, and French Knots.

The design was stitched over two fabric threads on a 45" x 58" piece of ivory, all-cotton, Anne Cloth (18 ct).

For afghan, cut off selvages of fabric; measure 5$^1/_2$" from raw edge of fabric and pull out one fabric thread. Fringe fabric up to missing fabric thread. Repeat for each side.

Tie an overhand knot at each corner using four horizontal and four vertical fringed threads. Working from corners, use eight fabric threads for each knot until all fringed threads are knotted.

Refer to Placement Diagram, page 173, for placement of design on fabric; use six strands of floss for *Cross Stitch* and two strands for *Backstitch* and *French Knots*.

Framed Cross-Stitched Santa

Refer to Cross Stitch, page 185, while working project. Follow the chart and stitch key, page 174. Use three strands of floss for Cross Stitch and one strand for Half Cross Stitch, Backstitch, and French Knots.

Stitch design over two fabric threads on a 13" x 14" piece of ivory Lugana (25 ct). Our finished piece was custom framed.

ST. NICOLAS PILLOW

(shown on page 28)

You will need photo transfer paper, 7" x 7" piece of muslin, Steam-A-Seam 2® Double Stick iron on fusible web, $^3/_4$"w ribbon, two 4"h x 7"w pieces of chenille for top and bottom borders, 40g of clear micro beads, brayer, hot glue gun, cording and coordinating corded tassel, two 6$^1/_4$"w x 13"h pieces of red patterned fabric for side borders and one 13"h x 17$^1/_2$"w piece for pillow back, 1"-long red fringe with decorative flange, and polyester fiberfill.

Match right sides and raw edges and use a $^1/_2$" seam allowance for all sewing.

1. For center piece, follow manufacturer's instructions to make a color photocopy of Santa, page 172, on transfer paper. Transfer Santa to center of muslin piece. Use fusible web to attach lengths of ribbon around Santa.
2. For pillow front, sew top and bottom borders to center piece.
3. Cut a piece of fusible web the size of Santa and ribbon borders. Remove one side of web paper and adhere to Santa; remove paper from remaining side, then pour beads onto the surface. Use brayer to smooth beads onto surface, adding beads as necessary to cover entire surface.
4. Follow the manufacturer's instructions to fuse beads to the surface.

5. Glue a length of cording along seams of center piece.
6. Sew side borders to each side of center panel.
7. Glue fringe along seams of center panel; glue cording on fringe.
8. Leaving an opening for turning, sew pillow front and back pieces together; clip corners, then turn right side out. Stuff pillow with fiberfill, then sew opening closed.
9. Tack tassel in place and tie into a bow.

HOLIDAY CLOCK

(shown on page 28)

You will need wood glue; wooden appliqués; wooden clock; sandpaper; tack cloth; primer; paintbrushes; burnt umber, ivory, and red acrylic paint; tracing paper; transfer paper and stylus; spouncer; $^3/_{16}$" U-channel lead came; wire cutters; nail set, hammer, and small nails; white spray paint for plastic; red plastic bead garland, and a hot glue gun.

1. Use wood glue to attach appliqués to clock.
2. Sand clock, then wipe it with the tack cloth. Apply primer to clock.
3. Paint clock burnt umber, then paint it ivory. For an aged look, lightly sand clock, revealing some of the base coat; wipe with the tack cloth.
4. Type "It's That TIME of the Year" on a computer; print. Use transfer paper and stylus to transfer phrase to clock. Paint phrase with a mixture of one part burnt umber and two parts red paint.

5. Use the sponcer to paint feet of clock base with burnt umber, then with paint mixture. Paint clock hands red.

6. Measure along top of clock where lead came is to be attached, then cut a piece of came $^1/_8$" longer than the determined measurement.

7. With channel facing up, bend came to fit along top of clock. Using the nail set, hammer nails flush with bottom of channel to attach came.

8. Spray paint bead garland and hot glue it along came's channel. Lightly sand garland to reveal a small amount of red on beads.

FESTIVE APRON
(shown on pages 27 and 29)

You will need kraft paper, 1 yd. of fabric, fabric glue, trim, cording, tassel, and a beaded shank button.

Use a $^1/_4$" seam allowance for all sewing.

1. Referring to Apron Diagram, draw a pattern on kraft paper; cut out. Pin pattern to fabric as indicated, then cut out along pattern lines.

2. Make a hem (turning under twice) in edges of apron.

3. For ties, cut two 1" x 42" strips from fabric. For each tie, press one end of one strip $^1/_2$" to wrong side. Matching wrong sides, press strip in half lengthwise; unfold. Press long raw edges to center; refold and topstitch along edges.

4. For strap, cut a $2^1/_2$" x 25" strip from fabric. Matching wrong sides, press strip in half lengthwise; unfold. Press long raw edges to center; refold and topstitch along edges.

5. Sew ties and strap to apron.

6. For pocket, cut two $6^1/_2$" x 8" pieces from fabric. Matching right sides and leaving one short end open, sew pocket pieces together; clip corners diagonally. Turn pocket right side out and press raw edges to inside (top). Wrapping ends to back, glue trim along top of pocket, then topstitch pocket to apron along side and bottom edges.

7. Accent apron by gluing trim along top edge of apron; glue cording over trim. Attach tassel to pocket; stitch button over top of tassel.

Apron Diagram

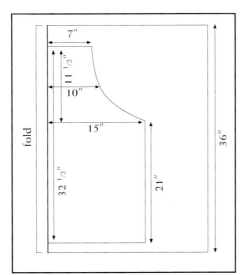

SANTA ORNAMENTS
(shown on pages 26 and 31)

For each ornament, you will need spray adhesive; 5" x 6" wooden rectangle cutout, $3^1/_4$" x $4^1/_2$" wooden rectangle cutout, or $2^3/_4$" x $4^1/_2$" wooden oval cutout; ribbon; double-stick self-adhesive sheets; 40g of clear micro beads; brayer; $^3/_8$" U-channel lead came; epoxy putty; plastic-coated pliers; $^1/_8$" dia. armature wire; hot glue gun; jingle bells; and acrylic jewels.

1. (*Note: For largest Santa ornament, cut lengths of ribbon for borders; use spray adhesive to secure ribbon, then Santa to cutout.*) For each ornament, make a color photocopy of a Santa picture from pages 172 and 173; cut out. Use spray adhesive to attach Santa to the cutout.

2. Draw around ornament on one side of an adhesive sheet, then cut out just inside drawn line.

3. Remove paper from one side of sheet and adhere to ornament; remove paper from remaining side, then pour beads onto the sheet. Use the brayer to smooth the beaded surface, adding beads as necessary to cover entire ornament.

4. Measure around ornament, then cut lead came the determined measurement. With channel of came facing in (covering edge of cutout), use epoxy to adhere came around ornament.

5. Use pliers to form armature wire into hanger. Use epoxy to adhere hanger to ornament; hot glue bells and jewels to top of ornament.

FABRIC-LINED BASKETS

(shown on pages 26 and 29)

Flat Basket Liner

Cut a square piece of fabric large enough to fit in basket and wrap to outside of basket; make a ¼" hem (turning under twice) in edges of fabric. Hot glue cording along top edges of fabric, then attach a tassel to one corner.

Fitted Basket Liners

For each basket liner, you will need a basket with handles; two coordinating fabrics; low-loft batting; hot glue gun; fringe or gimp, cording, tassel, and a button.

Use a ½" seam allowance for all sewing.

1. For inside sides liner, refer to Fig. 1 to measure around rim of basket (A); add 1". Measure from rim to center bottom of basket (B); add 1". Cut a piece of fabric the determined measurements.

Fig. 1

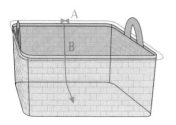

2. Matching right sides and short edges, sew fabric piece together. Press seam open; turn right side out. With seam at center back, place liner in basket and mark placement for handles (Fig. 2).

Fig. 2

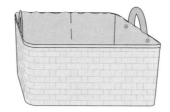

3. For cuff, measure around rim of basket (A); add 1". Cut a piece of fabric 7" by the determined measurement.
4. Matching wrong sides, fold fabric piece in half lengthwise. Matching short edges, sew piece together.
5. Matching raw edges and leaving openings for handles, pin cuff to liner. Sew cuff to liner, then turn liner and topstitch the raw edges of handle openings.
6. For bottom liner, cut two pieces of fabric and one piece of batting to fit in bottom of basket. Matching right sides and leaving an opening for turning, layer fabric, then batting and sew pieces together. Turn liner right side out and top stitch along edges, sewing opening closed.
7. Glue trim, then cording around the cuff and finish by adding the tassel and button.

CLOCK ORNAMENTS

(shown on pages 26 and 31)

For each ornament, you will need yellow paper, sayings rubber stamp and brown ink pad, spray adhesive, 2½" dia. wooden cutout, double-stick self-adhesive sheets, 40g of clear micro beads, brayer, wire cutters, ⅜" U-channel lead came, epoxy putty, hot glue gun, silver 20-gauge wire, large silver bead, silver bead garland, and a red ribbon bow.

Use hot glue for all gluing unless otherwise indicated.

1. Make a photocopy of the clock design, page 172, on yellow paper; cut out. Stamp words over design. Use spray adhesive to attach design to cutout.
2. Draw around clock on one side of an adhesive sheet, then cut out just inside drawn line.
3. Remove paper from one side of sheet and adhere to design; remove remaining paper, then pour beads onto sheet. Use the brayer to smooth the beaded surface, adding beads as necessary to cover entire surface.
4. Measure around clock, then cut lead came the determined measurement. With channel of came facing in (covering edge of cutout), use epoxy to adhere came around clock.
5. For hanger, glue twisted end of a loop of wire in a hole in silver bead; glue bead to top center of clock. Glue a length of bead garland to came.
6. Glue ribbon bow to top of ornament.

Tip French script scrapbooking paper is a great alternative to using a rubber stamp and ink pad to create the clock ornaments.

BEADED STOCKINGS
(shown on page 30)

For each stocking, you will need two 25" x 30" pieces red fabric for stocking, $^3/_8$" dia. welting, two 25" x 30" pieces cotton fabric for lining, 10" x 20" chenille fabric piece for cuff; 10" x 20" cotton fabric piece for cuff lining; 1"-long red fringe with decorative flange, two coordinating $^3/_{16}$" dia. decorative cordings, photo transfer paper, 6" x 8" piece of muslin for ornament, $3^1/_2$"h x $4^1/_2$"w oval piece of poster board, hot glue gun, Steam-A-Seam 2® Double Stick iron on fusible web, 40g of clear micro beads, brayer, and a corded tassel.

Use a $^1/_2$" seam allowance for all sewing.

1. Enlarge stocking pattern, page 175, 182%; cut out. Place right sides of stocking fabric pieces together and use pattern to cut out stocking.
2. Beginning and ending 1" from top edges of stocking and matching edges, pin flange of welting to right side of stocking front piece.
3. Matching right sides and leaving top edges open, sew stocking pieces together. Clip curves, then turn right side out.

4. For lining, place right sides of lining fabric pieces together; use pattern to cut out stocking lining. Matching right sides of fabric and leaving top edges open, sew stocking lining pieces together. Clip curves; do not turn right side out.
5. Insert lining into stocking. Baste lining to stocking along top edges.
6. For cuff, matching right sides and short edges of cuff fabric piece, sew short edges together; press seam open. Turn right side out.
7. For cuff lining, repeat Step 6 using cuff lining fabric piece; do not turn right side out.
8. Beginning and ending at seam line, pin flange of fringe along one edge (bottom) on right side of cuff.
9. For hanger, fold a 12" length of cording in half. With ends of cording extending $^1/_2$" beyond top edge of cuff, baste hanger to cuff at seam.
10. Matching right sides, bottom edges, and seam lines, place cuff lining over cuff; sew bottom edges together. Matching top edges, insert cuff into stocking.
11. Sew cuff to stocking. Turn cuff to outside.
12. For the Santa ornament, follow manufacturer's instructions to make a color photocopy of a Santa from page 172 or 173, on transfer paper. Transfer the Santa to center of muslin piece. Center the Santa on poster board, then wrap and glue edges of fabric to back.
13. Cut a piece of fusible web the size of the ornament. Remove one side of web paper and adhere to Santa; remove paper from remaining side, then pour the beads onto the surface. Use the brayer to smooth the beads onto the surface, adding beads as necessary to cover the entire surface.

14. Follow the manufacturer's instructions to fuse the beads to the ornament.
15. Glue the ornament to the cuff. Glue a length of cording around the ornament and a length along the edge of the fringe.
16. Tie tassel into a bow and glue to bottom of ornament.

PAINTED SHELF
(shown on page 30)

You will need glass doorknobs with the shafts removed, wooden appliqués, decorative wooden shelf (ours measures $47^1/_2$"-long), drill and drill bit the dia. of the bolts, wood glue, burnt umber and ivory acrylic paint, paintbrushes, sandpaper, tack cloth, bolts to fit snugly in doorknobs, and glue for metal.

1. Arrange doorknobs and appliqués on shelf, then mark their placement. Drill holes for doorknobs. Glue appliqués to shelf.
2. Paint shelf burnt umber, then paint it ivory. Lightly sand shelf to create an aged look, revealing some of the base coat; wipe with the tack cloth.
3. Working from back to front, push a bolt through each hole. Use metal glue to adhere doorknobs to bolts.

Season of Serenity

Choose your favorite supplies to create original gifts, decorations, and other Christmas keepsakes.
We're providing a few of our favorite embellishment ideas to inspire you.

Embellishing Ideas

Make multiples of one kind of card at the same time so you'll always have one on hand.

Use alphabet stickers in place of hand-lettering.

Knot a length of raffia to form an "O."

To add interest, mix upper and lower case letters to spell a word.

Use color ink to print letters/words.

Use embroidery floss to sew buttons or charms to card stock.

Glue buttons to ends of leaves for berries.

Use a single button as an "O."

To make paper appear aged, spray it with glossy wood-tone spray.

To emphasize words: type them in a different type style, use the phonetic spelling as printed in the dictionary, handwrite on aged paper, or photocopy the alphabet patterns from page 163.

Glue buttons or faux pearls in the shape of a tree, wreath or letter on card stock.

Use raffia, cinnamon sticks, string, dried fruit, buttons, photocopies of letters, and twigs to letter tags.

Use a felt-tip marker to write letters on leaves.

Cut letters from magazines in different types to capitalize or spell out a word.

Use a sewing machine or hand stitch over hand-lettered words.

Use a computer to print out words, leaving extra space between each letter, then cut out each letter.

Supply List

Embellishments
- cinnamon sticks
- dried apples
- miniature pinecones
- paper flowers
- artificial or dried flowers and greenery
- twigs and stems
- dried or preserved leaves
- buttons
- faux pearls
- jingle bells
- feathers
- string
- raffia
- ribbon
- craft wire
- embroidery floss
- charms

Papers
- decorative and handmade papers
- dictionary scrapbooking papers or pages from an old dictionary
- card stock
- corrugated paper
- blank cards and envelopes
- tissue paper

Lettering
- rubber stamps and ink pads
- paint pens
- permanent fine-point markers
- felt-tip markers
- printed or photocopied letters and words
- stickers
- magazine cutouts
- stencils

Accessories
- metal-rimmed tags
- wooden cargo tags
- eyelets
- paper fasteners

Adhesives
- spray adhesive
- tacky glue
- self-adhesive foam spacers
- double-sided tape
- hot glue

Tools
- hole punches
- eyelet setters
- wire cutters
- craft knife and cutting mat
- decorative-edge craft scissors
- straight-edge scissors

PAPIER-MÂCHÉ ORNAMENTS

(shown on page 33)

You will need an old dictionary, glossy wood-tone spray, sponge brush, découpage glue, $2^{1}/_{2}$" dia. and $3^{1}/_{2}$" dia. papier-mâché ornaments, photocopies of words spelled from alphabet patterns (page 163), hot glue gun, Tiny Tags (this page), and items from the Supply List (page 140).

1. Tear several pages from dictionary. For an aged look, spray pages with wood-tone spray.
2. Tear pages into small pieces, then using sponge brush and overlapping edges, follow *Découpaging*, page 185, to attach pieces to ornaments, covering surface as desired.
3. Follow *Découpaging*, page 185, to attach photocopied letters.
4. Using hot glue, embellish ornaments by adding Tiny Tags and items from the Supply List.

TINY TAG TREE

(shown on page 32)

You will need a hot glue gun, plastic floral foam blocks, $6^{1}/_{2}$"h jadite vase, small artificial tree (ours is 24"h), sheet moss, and assorted sizes of Tiny Tags (this page).

1. Layer and glue foam pieces together, then trim foam to fit snuggly in vase.
2. Insert tree into center of the foam, then cover foam with moss.
3. Tie Tiny Tags to limbs of tree.

TINY TAGS

(shown on pages 32 – 39)

You will need card stock; tacky glue; decorative paper; items from the Supply List (page 140); hole punch; and string, ribbon, or raffia.

1. Cut $^{1}/_{2}$" x 1" to 2" x $3^{3}/_{4}$" size tags from card stock; trim corners from one end.
2. For layered tags, glue a slightly smaller tag cut from decorative paper to the card stock tag.
3. Using items suggested in the Supply List and referring to our Embellishing Ideas on page 140, embellish tags.
4. To hang, punch a hole through top of tag, then attach string, ribbon, or raffia.

MEMORY ALBUM

(shown on page 38)

You will need mat board, assorted colors of decorative paper, card stock, tacky glue, craft knife and cutting mat, handmade paper, $^{1}/_{4}$" dia. grommets and a grommet kit, 6" x 9" white envelopes, hole punch, $^{1}/_{4}$" dia. reinforcement stickers, $1^{3}/_{4}$" x 3" Tiny Tag (this page), items from Supply List (page 140), two 1" dia. card stock circles, string, paper fasteners, and three hinged rings.

1. For covers, cut two $6^{1}/_{4}$" x $9^{1}/_{2}$" pieces from mat board and two pieces from decorative paper. Adhere paper pieces to one side of mat board pieces.
2. For front cover, use craft knife and cutting mat to cut a rectangle in one mat board near bottom edge. Cut a piece of card stock to fit inside front cover, then glue it in place.
3. Glue a torn piece of handmade paper along left side of front cover.
4. Mark placement for grommets on front and back covers; attach grommets.
5. Mark placements for holes in closed end of envelopes; punch holes. Adhere reinforcement stickers over one or both sides of holes.
6. Decorate cover referring to Embellishment Ideas (page 140), using Tiny Tag, elements from the Framed Pieces (page 142) and items from the Supply List.
7. Label envelope fronts.
8. For envelope closure, refer to Fig. 1 to make a small hole through one circle of card stock and in envelope flap. Knot a length of string on inside of flap; thread string through hole in flap, then circle; tie string into a bow close to circle. Use paper fastener to attach second circle of card stock to back of envelope, just below flap. Wrap tail of bow around closure to secure.

Fig. 1

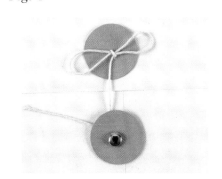

9. Place envelopes between front and back covers, then slip rings through holes.

FRAMED PIECES

(shown on pages 34, 36, and 37)

You will need assorted sizes of frames with backings for Framed Words and an 11½" x 21½" frame with backing for Large Framed Collage; assorted colors of paint; paintbrushes; poster board; spray adhesive; decorative papers; Tiny Tags (page 141); wooden tags; ribbon, string, or raffia; photocopies of words spelled from alphabet patterns (page 163); items from the Supply List (page 140); mat board; dictionary scrapbooking papers or pages from an old dictionary; brown tissue paper; twigs; buttons; alphabet stencils; felt-tip markers; tacky glue; craft wire; card stock; embroidery floss; photo corners; corrugated paper; craft knife and cutting mat; dried apple slices; cinnamon sticks; and artificial greenery.

Framed Words

1. For each frame, remove backing. Apply a basecoat, then accent frame with a second color of paint.
2. Cut a piece of poster board to fit in frame. For background, use spray adhesive to adhere decorative paper to poster board, then secure background and backing in frame.
3. Embellish background by adding tags tied with ribbon, string, or raffia, photocopies of words spelled from alphabet patterns, or words spelled from raffia.
4. Accent tags and embellish frames using items from the Supply List and inspiration from the Embellishing Ideas, page 140.

Large Framed Collage

1. Remove backing, then cut a piece of mat board to fit in frame.
2. Use spray adhesive to adhere decorative paper, dictionary paper, then tissue paper to mat board for background. Secure background and backing in frame.
3. For the "PEACE" tags, follow Steps 1, 2 and 4 of Tiny Tags to make five 1⅞" x 3" tags. Use twigs, string, raffia, buttons, and a stencil and marker to shape one letter on each tag; glue shaped letters in place. Glue tags to collage. Use craft wire to attach ½" x 1¼" tags labeled with "faith," "hope," and "love" to the hangers of the "P," "A," and "E" tags.
4. Use a pencil to lightly write the word "Harmony" on a piece of card stock, then use three strands of floss to work backstitches over the word. Accent the corners of the stitched piece with photo corners, then glue it to a coordinating piece of card stock.
5. For the "WORLD" frames, cut five 2¼" x 3" pieces from corrugated paper, three 2¼" x 3" pieces from one color card stock and two 2¼" x 3" pieces from another color card stock. Using the craft knife and cutting mat, cut out a 1½" x 1¾" section from the center of each corrugated paper piece. Stack pieces to form frames, alternating between the colored card stock centers. Type "WORLD" in a computer document, then cut out each letter just outside the lines. Glue the letters to the frames.

6. Embellish collage with dried apple slices formed into heart shapes, raffia bows, or cinnamon sticks wrapped with craft wire…we used craft wire to attach a piece of artificial greenery and a button to our cinnamon stick.
7. Refer to photo on page 34, Embellishing Ideas on page 140, and use items from the Supply List to help you create your collage.

CREATIVE CARDS

(shown on page 39)

You will need items from the Supply List (page 140), assorted sizes of cards and envelopes, self-adhesive foam spacers, ribbon, card stock, tacky glue, raffia, craft knife and cutting mat, and decorative paper.

Referring to Embellishing Ideas (page 140) and the photo on page 39 for inspiration, decorate cards and envelopes using items from the Supply List.

For the "Harmony" card, we used self-adhesive foam spacers to raise the paper with the word "Harmony."

For the "Peace" card, we mitered ribbon at corners to form a frame around center piece of card stock.

For the "Joy" card, we glued lengths of raffia around card stock, before gluing it to card front, then added a raffia bow.

For the square card, we used a craft knife and cutting mat to cut out six small squares for "frames," then we glued a lighter piece of decorative paper to inside of card.

REINDEER
(shown on pages 32 and 36)

For each reindeer, you will need aluminum foil, approx. three (five) 2 oz. packages of modeling clay, 18-gauge wire, pliers, four 3¹/₂"-long (4¹/₂"-long) craft sticks, découpage glue, foam brush, off-white handmade paper, brown and black acrylic paint and paintbrushes, two black seed beads, small charm, and raffia.

Our reindeer measure 6"-long x 3¹/₂"h (5"h to top of head) and 8³/₄"-long x 5"h (6¹/₄"h to top of head).

Note that the large reindeer measurement information will be indicated in parentheses following the information for the small reindeer.

1. Referring to Reindeer Table and Fig. 1, form pieces from crumpled foil and clay for reindeer body.

Fig. 1

2. For each antler, cut one 2" (3") and one 2¹/₂" (3¹/₂") length of wire. Twist wires together to form antler (Fig. 1, above).

3. For legs, trim craft sticks to 2¹/₂"-long (4"-long).
4. Wrap flattened clay piece around foil body and smooth edges to cover foil. Add neck and head, smoothing clay in place and shaping head and neck into desired position.
5. Insert ¹/₂" of each leg into body. Insert antlers into head (Fig. 2).

Fig. 2

6. Referring to Fig. 3, cover antlers and legs with clay. Shape a tail and two ears from clay and attach to body. Add and smooth clay to areas to mold and shape reindeer.

Fig. 3

7. Follow manufacturer's instructions to bake reindeer and nose.
8. (*Note:* We used a contrasting color of handmade paper for our photo.) Refer to Fig. 4 for *Découpaging*, page 185, the reindeer with torn pieces of handmade paper.

Fig. 4

9. Paint brown hooves and nose black. Glue bead eyes and nose to reindeer.
10. Thread charm onto a length of raffia, then tie it around the reindeer's neck (Fig. 5).

Fig. 5

REINDEER TABLE

PART	SHAPE	SMALL DEER	LARGE DEER
		from crumpled foil:	
body	cylinder	3³/₄" long x 1¹/₄" dia.	5" long x 1¹/₂" dia.
		from clay:	
skin	flat	5" x 6"	7" x 7"
neck	drum	1" long x 1" dia.	1¹/₂" long x 1¹/₂" dia.
head	cone	2" long	2¹/₂" long
nose	heart	⁵/₁₆"w	⁷/₁₆"w

Ranch Hand Roundup

GIFT TAGS
(shown on page 42)

For each tag, you will need yellow and green card stock, craft glue stick, 1/4" dia. hole punch, 1/2" dia. star punch, and twine.

1. Cut a cargo-style tag from the yellow card stock. Draw around tag on green card stock, then cut out 1/4" outside drawn lines.
2. Center and glue the yellow tag to the green tag, then punch a hole in tag.
3. Punch three green stars; glue stars to tag.
4. Write name on tag, then use twine to attach tag to gift.

BANDANNA GARLAND
(shown on pages 41 and 42)

You will need bandannas.

1. Cut bandannas into four squares.
2. Forming a triangle, fold squares in half.
3. Knot the unfinished ends of two triangles together. Continue adding triangles until desired length is reached.

TEN-GALLON TREE TOPPER
(shown on page 41)

You will need a red bandanna, cowboy hat, double-stick foam spacer, and a large Painted Wooden Star (this page).

1. Forming a triangle, fold the bandanna in half, then roll it from the long end toward the point; knot it around the hat.
2. Adhere the spacer to the back of the star, then stick it on the hat.

PAINTED WOODEN STARS
(shown on pages 40 and 47)

You will need 1 1/2" and 3" dia. wooden star appliques; yellow, dark yellow, red, and dark red acrylic paints; paintbrushes; and optional: hot glue gun and craft wire or 1/2" or 3/4" dia. magnets.

1. For each yellow star, paint the inside of the star yellow, then paint every other triangle dark yellow. Paint the border red.
2. For each red star, paint the inside of the star red, then paint every other triangle dark red. Paint the border yellow.

Star Ornaments: Glue the ends of a loop of wire to the back of a Painted Star.

Star Magnets: Glue a magnet to the back of a Painted Star.

CHRISTMAS COWBELLS
(shown on pages 42 and 46)

For each small ornament, attach a small Painted Wooden Star Magnet, (this page), to a 2 1/4"h cowbell. For each large ornament, attach a large Painted Wooden Star Magnet (this page) to a 4"h cowbell. For each hanger, tie a length of ribbon into a bow around the bell handle.

PAINTED PONY TREE SKIRT
(shown on page 42)

You will need tracing paper, muslin, denim, brown paint, paintbrush or craft sponge, fabric glue, brown suede fringe, and red trim.

Use a 1/4" seam allowance for all sewing.

1. Using tree skirt section patterns A, B, C, and D, pages 176 and 177, and following *Making Patterns*, page 184, make a whole tree skirt section pattern on tracing paper; cut out.
2. Draw around pattern six times on muslin and six times on denim; cut out.
3. Paint a brown pony print on each muslin section.
4. Alternating fabrics and matching right sides, sew sections together along long edges. Hem raw edges and press seams to one side.
5. Glue fringe along edges of skirt, then glue trim on flange of fringe.

DECORATED DRINKING GLASSES

(shown on pages 41 and 44)

You will need drinking glasses, 1"w red and white striped ribbon, hot glue gun, and small Painted Wooden Stars (page 144).

1. For each glass, measure around glass where the ribbon will be placed; add ¹/₂". Cut a length of ribbon the determined measurement.
2. Wrap ribbon around glass, then glue the ends together. Glue a star over the overlap.

COWBOY BOOT ORNAMENTS

(shown on pages 41 and 43)

You will need tracing paper, transfer paper and stylus, faux suede, assorted acrylic paints, paintbrushes, assorted colors of paint pens, ¹/₄" dia. grommets and a grommet setter, and craft wire.

1. (Note: Reverse pattern for red boots. Transfer stitching pattern on toe to red and blue boots and holly pattern to green boots.) For each ornament, trace the boot pattern, page 178, onto tracing paper. Transfer design to suede; cut out.
2. Refer to photos, page 43 and above, to paint desired boot.
3. Use pen to draw pen-stitching and add details to boot.
4. Follow the manufacturer's instructions to attach a grommet to the top of boot.
5. For hanger, thread a length of wire through grommet; twist ends together to secure.

CARD HOLDERS

(shown on pages 44 and 46)

You will need a pushpin; 1¹/₂" and 1¹/₄" square wooden blocks; yellow, red, green, and black acrylic paint; paintbrushes; hot glue gun; varying lengths of green 18-gauge wire; Painted Wooden Stars (page 144); ¹/₂" and ³/₄" dia. magnets; yellow, red, and green card stock; craft glue stick; and a black marker.

Place Card Holders

1. For each holder, use the pushpin to make a hole in the top center of a 1¹/₄" block.
2. Paint the front of the block yellow and the remaining sides of the block red or green.
3. Glue one end of a length of wire to the back of a small Painted Wooden Star.
4. Stack two coordinating magnets together, then glue stack to the back of the star. Glue remaining end of wire in hole in block.
5. Cut a 1¹/₂" x 2¹/₂" piece from yellow card stock, then a 1³/₄" x 2³/₄" piece from red or green card stock. Use the glue stick to adhere yellow piece onto the red or green piece, then write the name on the card.
6. Place card between magnets.

Christmas Card Holders

1. Follow Steps 1 and 2 of Place Card Holders to make fourteen blocks.
2. Using black paint and alternating block colors, spell out "MERRY CHRISTMAS" on the fronts of the blocks.
3. Follow Steps 3 and 4 of Place Card Holders to add six large and eight small Painted Wooden Stars to the blocks.
4. Place Christmas cards between magnets.

COWBOY HAT ORNAMENTS

(shown on pages 41 and 43)

You will need brown and red 5"-long flocked cowboy hats, hot glue gun, bandanna print ribbon, miniature artificial holly leaves with berry clusters, ¹/₈" dia. hole punch and ¹/₂" dia. star punch, leather lacing, red trim, and yellow and green card stock.

1. For brown hat, remove leather lacing and glue a length of ribbon around hat. Glue holly leaf and berry cluster to hat.
2. For red hat, glue a holly leaf and berry cluster to hat.
3. To hang hats, punch a hole on each side of hat. Knotting ends on inside of hat, thread a length of lacing or trim through holes.
4. For stars, punch a star in one color card stock, then glue the star to remaining color card stock and cut out just outside star.

Tip Flocked cowboy hats can be found in the doll accessory area of your local craft store. They are available in several colors, or you can use spray paint to paint them to match your décor.

HORSESHOE CANDLEHOLDERS

(shown on page 44)

For each candleholder, you will need four same-size horseshoes, detergent, wire cutters, four 4" lengths of 16 gauge galvanized wire, rust-colored metal primer, red spray paint for metal, craft glue, artificial holly springs, jar to fit in horseshoe ring, braided sisal rope, and a candle to fit in jar.

1. Clean horseshoes with detergent.
2. Working from front to back, thread ends of wire though side holes in two horseshoes. Twist wire together at back, then bend wire flat against one horseshoe. Forming a ring, repeat until all four horseshoes are wired together.
3. Prime, then paint the horseshoe ring red.
4. Glue holly sprigs to horseshoes.
5. Measure around jar threads; double measurement, then add 1/2"; cut a length of rope the determined measurement. Wrap and glue rope around threads, trimming ends to meet.
6. Place candle in jar, then jar in horseshoe ring.

STAR TABLE TOPPER

(shown on page 45)

You will need fusible web, muslin, brown acrylic paint, paintbrush or craft sponge, 40" square of denim, fabric glue, brown suede fringe, and red trim.

1. Using star point pattern, page 176, and matching green lines, follow Steps 1 and 2 of *Fusible Appliqués*, page 185, to make star appliqué from muslin; cut out.

2. Paint brown pony print on the star appliqué.
3. Center and fuse the star appliqué to the denim piece.
4. Mark a point on denim 4" outside each inner point, then mark a point 6" outside each outer point. Using a straight edge, connect the points; cut out denim star.
5. Glue fringe along edges of denim star, then glue trim along edges of star appliqué and to flange of fringe.

HORSESHOE STOCKING HOLDERS

(shown on page 47)

For each stocking holder, you will need a large horseshoe for the base and a small horseshoe for the hook, detergent, wire cutters, 16-gauge galvanized wire, rust-colored metal primer, and red spray paint for metal.

1. Clean horseshoes with detergent.
2. With the large horseshoe as the base and twisting the wire so it rests on top of the large horseshoe, wire the shoes together through their bottom holes.
3. Prime, then paint the stocking holder red.

ROOTIN' TOOTIN' WREATH

(shown on page 46)

You will need fresh greenery, floral picks, hot glue gun, grapevine wreath, sisal rope, three small Christmas Cowbells with hangers and three large Christmas Cowbells without hangers (page 144), 1"w red and white striped ribbon, Painted Wooden Stars (page 144), and a red bandanna.

1. After attaching greenery to floral picks, arrange and glue the picks in the wreath until desired coverage is achieved.
2. Gluing the rope ends together at back of wreath, hang large Christmas Cowbells from varying lengths of rope around the bottom of the wreath.
3. Gluing at back, wrap the ribbon around the wreath. Form a lasso-like loop in one end of a length of rope and glue it in place, then wrap the remainder of the rope around the wreath.
4. Glue the Painted Wooden Stars to the wreath and hang the small Christmas Cowbells from the wreath.
5. Fold the bandanna in half and tie it around the wreath.

CANDY CANE BOUQUET

(shown on page 47)

You will need a cowboy boot, tracing paper, transfer paper and stylus, assorted acrylic paints, paintbrushes, rocks, Oasis® floral foam, tall glass to fit in boot for liner, fresh greenery, candy canes, floral tape, and floral picks.

Refer to Assembling Arrangement, next page, to help you create your arrangement.

1. Clean boot as necessary.
2. Trace and transfer holly and star patterns, page 177, onto boot, then paint boot as desired.
3. To weight boot, fill bottom of boot with rocks. Soak foam in water, then place in liner. Place liner in boot, then arrange greenery in foam until desired look is achieved.
4. Wrap the base of each candy cane with tape, then attach it to a floral pick and insert it into the foam.

BOOT CENTERPIECE
(shown on pages 41 and 45)

For each arrangement, you will need a cowboy boot, tracing paper, transfer paper and stylus, red and assorted acrylic paints, paintbrushes, small wooden balls, hot glue gun, Painted Wooden Stars (page 144), rocks (optional), Oasis® floral foam, container to fit in boot for liner, fresh greenery and berry twigs, wire cutters, various lengths of 16-guage floral wire, and a red bandanna for standing arrangement.

Refer to Assembling Arrangement, this page, to help you create your arrangement.

1. Clean boot as necessary.
2. Trace and transfer star pattern, page 178, to front of boot, then paint designs on boot as desired.
3. Paint wooden balls red, then glue to boot.
4. Glue a small Painted Wooden Star to each boot strap.
5. If needed to weight, fill the bottom of the boot with rocks. Soak foam in water, then place in liner. Place liner in boot, then arrange greenery in foam until desired look is achieved.
6. Glue wire lengths to the back of large stars and insert into foam as desired.
7. Tuck the bandanna in the standing arrangement.

Tip To keep greenery fresh during the holidays, lightly spritz it daily with water. Replace any withering greenery with fresh sprigs as needed.

ASSEMBLING ARRANGEMENTS

It is important when assembling decorative arrangements to create a visual balance between the different kinds and sizes of flowers, greenery, and/or decorative items used.

Place tall items at back of arrangements. Arrange focal items, then fill areas between items with medium-size and small items. To add short-stemmed items or small items to a foam-based arrangements, either wrap wire of a wired floral pick around an inconspicuous area of item or tape or glue pick to item.

COWBOY STOCKINGS
(shown on pages 41 and 47)

For each stocking, you will need transfer paper, stylus, faux leather, paper-backed fusible web, denim, 6"square of green felt, 14" x 18" piece of red felt, red thread (use for all sewing), pinking sheers, hot glue gun, and a large Painted Wooden Star (page 144).

1. Enlarge boot and denim patterns, page 178, 197%. Transfer the boot pattern to the wrong side of the leather; cut out.
2. Follow Steps 1 – 3 of *Fusible Appliqués*, page 185, to make each denim appliqué and three holly appliqués from green felt. Fuse denim appliqués to the boot.
3. Sew a double seam along the top edge of boot. Beginning just below top denim appliqué, sew a double seam down center of boot.
4. Fuse holly appliqués to boot. Sew a double seam down center of each leaf, then topstitch along edges of leaves.
5. Topstitch along remaining edges of denim appliqués. Referring to photo on page 47, stitch three lines across toe of boot.
6. Center boot on red felt; pin in place. Using pinking sheers, cut out felt ¹/₂" outside edges of boot. Leaving top of stocking open, sew pieces together.
7. For hanger, cut a 3" x 7" strip of denim and fusible web. Adhere web to wrong side of denim; remove paper backing, fold long edges to center, then press. Sew a double seam down both edges of strip. Matching wrong sides and ends, fold strip in half, then glue ends together. Glue hanger ends inside stocking.
8. Glue star to stocking.

Wrap It Up!

RIBBON DISPENSER

(shown on page 50)

You will need spray primer, spray paint, shoebox large enough to accommodate ribbon spools with lid on (ours measures 11³/₄" x 8" x 4³/₄"), eyelet charm tags for scrapbooking, craft knife, eyelets to fit charm tags and eyelet setter, The Ultimate! glue by Crafter's Pick™, two doll pin stands, craft saw, ³/₈" dia. dowel, spools of ribbon, and ribbon to glue to lid.

Our dispenser holds spools of ribbon that are 4" in diameter or less.

1. Prime, then paint entire box and lid.
2. Using tags as a pattern and using a craft knife for cutting, cut out openings in one side of box. Following manufacturer's instructions, attach eyelets to tags. Glue tags over holes.
3. To hold dowel, glue base of one doll pin stand to inside center on one side of box. Cut remaining doll pin stand in half vertically and glue base of half directly across box from doll pin stand.
4. Thread ribbon spools onto dowel, then place one end of dowel into hole in doll pin stand and rest remaining end in doll pin stand half.
5. Feed ribbon ends through holes in box.
6. Glue a length of ribbon along sides of box lid.

WOODEN GIFT TAGS

(shown on page 52)

For each tag, you will need a light and dark shade of desired color acrylic paint, paintbrushes, wooden gift tag, coordinating color ink pad, rubber stamp, clear embossing powder, heating tool, black permanent fine-point marker, craft glue, coordinating color ultra-fine glitter, small glitter stars, and coordinating ribbon.

1. Paint front and back of tag the light paint color. Paint edges of tag the dark paint color.
2. Using ink pad, stamp tag with rubber stamp. While ink is still wet, sprinkle tag with embossing powder; tap off any excess powder. Following heating tool manufacturer's instructions, emboss stamped area.
3. Using dark paint color, paint details on stamped design.
4. For back of tag, use dark paint color to paint "To:" and "From:". Use marker to write names.
5. Brush glue on front of tag, then sprinkle glitter on glue; allow to dry, then shake off any excess glitter. Repeat on back of tag. Glue stars to tags.
6. Use a length of ribbon to attach tag to gift.

STAMPED GIFT WRAP

(shown on page 51)

You will need tracing paper, 3mm craft foam sheets, hot glue gun, gift boxes large enough to accommodate stamps, paintbrushes, acrylic paint, white craft paper, and a pencil with a new eraser.

1. For holly or star stamps, trace patterns onto tracing paper; cut out. Draw around patterns onto craft foam; cut out.
2. Arrange, then glue holly or stars to bottom of gift box.
3. For tree stamp, trace tree pattern onto tracing paper; cut out. Draw around tree pattern onto bottom of gift box. Cut a ¹/₈"w x 15¹/₄"-long piece of craft foam. Using the drawn tree pattern as a guide, glue strip to bottom of gift box.
4. Brush paint onto stamps and stamp paper.
5. For holly berries and tree ornaments, dip the eraser end of pencil in paint and stamp paper.

WRAP IT UP ORGANIZER
(shown on page 51)

You will need red, gold, and green felt; corrugated cardboard; wire clothes hanger; spray adhesive; duct tape; fabric glue; tracing paper; beading needle and thread; six red sequins; six red miracle beads; six red 4mm beads; $2^1/2$"w gold sheer wire-edged ribbon; gold braid trim; 24" length of red eyelash fringe; pushpin; four buttons; and red chenille yarn.

1. Cut two 21" x 36" pieces from red felt and one 20" x 36" piece from cardboard.
2. Referring to Fig. 1, place hanger at top of cardboard piece and draw along top of hanger; cut cardboard along drawn lines.

Fig. 1

3. Center cardboard piece on one felt piece. Draw around cardboard piece on felt; cut out felt $1/4$" outside drawn lines. Repeat for remaining felt piece.

4. Use duct tape to secure hanger to cardboard piece.
5. Use spray adhesive to adhere one felt piece to each side of cardboard piece. Glue edges of felt together around cardboard piece.
6. For gold pouch, cut one $9^3/4$" x 21" piece from gold felt.
7. Trace holly leaf pattern, page 180, onto tracing paper; cut out. Use pattern to cut twelve holly leaves from green felt.
8. For holly pockets, stack two of each same-size leaf together. Using a zig-zag stitch, sew each stack of leaves together along edges. Positioning leaves on large pocket as indicated in photo on page 51 and leaving an opening for storage in two leaves, sew holly pockets to pouch.
9. For each holly berry, bring thread up through felt, then thread one sequin, one miracle bead, and one 4mm bead onto thread. Go back down through miracle bead, sequin, and fabric, then secure thread.
10. For package pocket, cut two 6" squares from red felt. Stack and pin squares together, then wrapping ends to back of stack, pin lengths of ribbon in place across squares. Using a zig-zag stitch, sew squares together. Leaving top open, sew package pocket to pouch.
11. Matching side edges, position pouch on red felt and glue in place on each side. Form a tuck at each corner and glue it in place, then glue bottom edge of pouch in place.
12. Glue trim along top edge of pouch, then mitering corners, glue trim along all outside edges of organizer. Glue trim to fringe.

13. Use pushpin to punch two holes through each side of organizer and one at center for fringe. For each set of holes, place one button at back of organizer and sewing through holes and buttons at back of organizer, sew fringe to organizer.
14. Use pushpin to punch two holes at top center of pouch. Place button at back of organizer and sewing though holes and button at back, tack pouch center to organizer.
15. Glue remaining holly leaves to top of organizer.
16. Gluing to secure, wrap exposed hanger with yarn.

COLOR-BLOCKED SHIRT BOX
(shown on page 52)

You will need two 12" square sheets each of two coordinating shades of vellum; shirt box; vellum tape; 1"w satin, $5/8$"w grosgrain, and $1/16$"w silk ribbon; three oval tags; stickers; fine-point permanent pen; and craft glue.

1. Cutting vellum to fit box, use tape to cover box top as desired.
2. Wrapping ends to inside of box and taping to secure, use satin and grosgrain ribbon to cover paper "seams."
3. For tags, attach stickers and write names on tags. Thread a length of $1/16$" dia. ribbon through each tag, then knot ribbon above tag. Glue ends to box under ribbon.

FESTIVE BOWS

(shown on page 53)

Poinsettia Bow

You will need 1⁵/₈"w wire-edged ribbon, 26-gauge floral wire, thirteen gold 8mm beads, three 2¹/₂" lengths of chenille stem, and a hot glue gun.

1. Follow *Multi-Loop Bow*, page 152, to make a six-loop bow with 8" loops and 1" streamers and a four-loop bow with 2³/₄" loops and ¹/₂" streamers.
2. Use wire to attach small bow to center of large bow.
3. For flower center, thread one bead to center of each chenille stem. Fold each stem in half and twist ends together to secure bead. Twist stems together, forming flower center. Glue flower center to center of bow.
4. For each loop, gather end of loop, sew a bead to each end.
5. Use wire ends to attach poinsettia bow to package.

Angel Bow

You will need 2¹/₂"w wire-edged ribbon for dress and head, 1³/₈"w wire-edged ribbon for wings, one chenille stem, ¹/₈"w ribbon, and a charm.

1. For dress, cut three 10" lengths of ribbon. Gathering ends, wrap center of chenille stem around ends; glue to secure.

2. For head, cut one 5" length of ribbon. Gathering ends, place ribbon ends behind dress and wrap chenille stem around ends; glue to secure.
3. For wings, cut one 12" length of ribbon. Overlapping ends and forming a loop, gather at the center, then place behind angel; wrap chenille stem around wings; glue to secure.
4. Use ¹/₈"w ribbon to attach charm at neck.
5. Use ends of chenille stem to attach angel bow to package.

Tree Bow

You will need 1⁵/₈"w wire-edged ribbon, 26-gauge floral wire, artificial greenery sprigs, and a hot glue gun.

1. For bottom bough, cut four 10" lengths of ribbon. Starting at one end of wire and gathering ribbon ends, twist wire around ends and greenery; glue to secure.
2. For next bough, cut three 6¹/₂" lengths of ribbon. Continuing to wrap with wire, gather ribbon ends and twist wire around ends and greenery; glue to secure.
3. For next bough, cut two 5" lengths of ribbon. Continuing to wrap with wire, gather ribbon ends and twist wire around ends and greenery; glue to secure.
4. For top bough, cut one 4³/₄" length of ribbon. Continuing to wrap with wire, gather ribbon ends and twist wire around ends; glue to secure.
5. Use hot glue to attach tree bow to package.

PLACEMAT WRAP

(shown on page 53)

You will need a placemat (we used a 14" x 20" chenille placemat), 1¹/₂"w wire-edged ribbon, and green embroidery floss.

1. Center, then sew one end of each 24" length of ribbon to wrong side of each long edge of placemat.
2. At each end, fold corners to center wrong side of placemat, forming a point. Use floss to tack ends together.
3. Referring to Fig. 1, bring the tacked corners to the point and tack in place.

Fig. 1

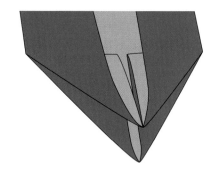

CHRISTMAS PHOTO KEEPER
(shown on page 54)

You will need a Christmas card, cigar box (ours measures $3^5/_8$" x $4^1/_2$" x $6^3/_4$" and has a sliding lid), craft glue, masking tape, acrylic paints and paintbrushes, mica snow, and color photocopy of alphabet on page 163.

1. Cut card to fit cigar box lid, still allowing lid to slide on and off. Glue card to lid.
2. Masking off along outer edges of each side of box with tape, paint box to coordinate with card background; once dry, remove tape.
3. Cover any areas on card (such as snow or Santa's beard and fur trim) with glue, then sprinkle with mica snow and allow to dry. Shake off any excess snow.
4. Cut out letters from alphabet to spell words or names and glue to sides of box. Apply glue along tops of letters, then sprinkle with mica snow and allow to dry. Shake off any excess snow.

RIBBON-TIED BOXES
(shown on page 54)

For each box, you will need tracing paper, poster board, craft knife, spray adhesive, fabric, paint pen to match fabric, eight eyelets and an eyelet setter, ribbon, and tissue paper.

You will need to enlarge or reduce square and pattern to fit gift.

1. Draw a $3^1/_2$" square onto center of poster board. Trace "triangle" pattern, page 179, onto tracing paper; cut out. Matching base of triangle with each side of square, draw around pattern onto poster board; cut out along outer drawn lines.
2. Carefully score box along fold lines, as indicated on pattern.
3. Spray one side of poster board with spray adhesive, then press poster board onto wrong side of fabric; cut out.
4. Use paint pen to paint outer edges poster board.
5. Following manufacturer's instructions, attach eyelets where indicated on pattern by a dot.
6. Lace ribbon through eyelets, pulling ribbon ends even at front.
7. Place gift item in tissue paper, then place in box. Pull ribbon taut and tie ribbon ends into a bow.

TERRIFIC TRIMMINGS
(shown on page 55)

Initial Wrapping Idea

You will need card stock, hot glue gun, letter rubber stamp, craft paint and paintbrush, shirt box, two coordinating tissue papers, double-sided tape, and $3/_4$"w ribbon.

1. Working on card stock while glue is hot, use stamp to imprint a quarter-sized dot of hot glue (leave stamp in glue until it cools).
2. Once cool, remove stamp and cut out close to glue dot.
3. Paint glue dot gold.
4. Place gift item in box; overlap two coordinating tissue papers at front to wrap item.

5. Use tape to attach a loop of ribbon to tissue paper at overlap.
6. Use tape to attach initial to center of ribbon loop.

Natural Wrapping Idea

You will need poster board, craft glue, $5/_8$"w ribbon, berry sprig, small pinecone, shirt box, and tissue paper.

1. Cut a 2" x 23" strip from poster board. Center and glue a length of ribbon to poster board strip.
2. Wrap gift in tissue paper, then wrap strip around gift and tape at back to secure. Place gift in box.
3. Glue sprig of berries and pinecone to center of poster board strip.

Stamped Ribbon Wrapping Idea

You will need a red ink pad, Christmas rubber stamp (our stamp reads "ho"), $5/_8$"w white ribbon, tissue paper, shirt box, craft glue, charm, thread, and double-sided tape.

1. Using red ink, stamp ribbon.
2. Wrap gift in tissue paper.
3. Taping at back, wrap gift with ribbon, horizontally and vertically. Place gift in box.
4. For bow, cut a 7" length of ribbon. Glue ends together forming a loop. For streamer, cut a $4^3/_4$" length of ribbon. Thread charm onto thread. With loop on top of streamer, tie thread around center of bow and streamer. Clip streamer ends.
5. Using tape, attach bow to gift.

Bows

HOW MUCH RIBBON DO YOU NEED?

To determine the amount of ribbon you will need for any size bow, follow this guide:

Diameter, in inches, you want the finished bow to be: _____ "
Multiply diameter by the number of loops you want: x _____ "
Add the length, in inches, of streamers (if any): + _____ "
Add an additional 6" to 12" for gathering and trimming: + _____ "
Divide by 36 to get the total ribbon yardage needed: _____ yds

SIMPLE BOW

1. For the first streamer, measure and lightly mark 10" from one end of ribbon. For the first loop, begin at streamer mark; measure and lightly mark 8".
2. To form first loop, place first loop mark behind streamer mark; gather ribbon between thumb and forefinger (Fig. 1).

Fig. 1

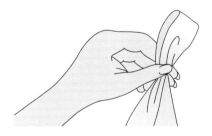

3. Loosely wrap remaining length of ribbon once around thumb (Fig. 2). To form second loop, fold remaining ribbon approximately 4" from end of wrapped area; slide folded end of ribbon through wrapped area.

Fig. 2

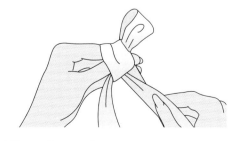

4. Place thumbs inside loops (Fig. 3). Pull the loops to tighten bow. Adjust size of loops by pulling on streamers. Trim streamers.

Fig. 3

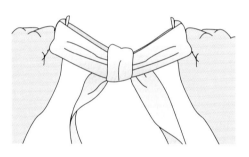

Simple Bow

MULTI-LOOP BOW

Note: Loop sizes given in project instructions refer to the length of ribbon used to make one loop of bow. If no size is given, make loops desired size for project.

1. For first streamer, measure desired length of streamer from one end of ribbon; twist ribbon between fingers (Fig. 1).

Fig. 1

2. Keeping right side of ribbon facing out, fold ribbon to front to form desired-size loop; gather ribbon between fingers (Fig. 2). Fold ribbon to back to form another loop; gather ribbon between fingers (Fig. 3).

Fig. 2

Fig. 3

3. (*Note:* If a center loop is desired, form half the desired number of loops, then loosely wrap ribbon around thumb and gather ribbon between fingers as shown in Fig. 4; form remaining loops.) Continue to form loops, varying size of loops as desired, until bow is desired size.

Fig. 4

4. For remaining streamer, trim ribbon to desired length.
5. To secure bow, hold gathered loops tightly. Fold a length of floral wire around gathers of loops. Hold wire ends behind bow, gathering all loops forward; twist bow to tighten wire. Arrange loops and trim ribbon ends as desired.

Multi-Loop Bow

Multi-Loop Bow with Center Loop

EASIEST BOW EVER (7" dia.)
1. Wrap ribbon lengthwise around a 4¹/₂" x 8¹/₂" piece of cardboard four times (Fig. 1).

Fig. 1

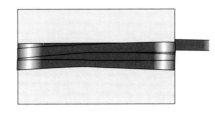

2. Use wire to secure each side of ribbon (Fig. 2).

Fig. 2

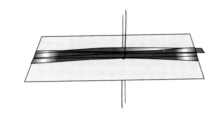

3. Slide ribbon off cardboard. Pinch ribbons together where wire meet (at center); use wires to secure bow (Fig. 3).

Fig. 3

4. Cut streamers and arrange loops.

Easiest Bow Ever

TRIMMING STREAMERS
Streamers may be trimmed in a variety of ways including angled, straight across, pointed, or notched. To notch or point a streamer end, fold the streamer in half lengthwise and cut at an angle from the folded edge to the open edge.

In some instances you may want to add a little fray preventative along the edges of the streamers to prevent fraying. Do so carefully, as not to saturate the ribbon.

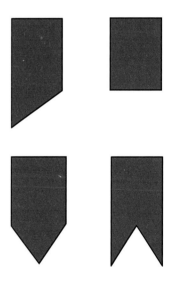

Gifts from Hand to Heart

GLASS FRAME PINS

(shown on page 56)

You will need a glass cutter, microscope slides, decorative paper for background, lace or other small decorative item to fit between slides, ¹/₄"w self-adhesive silvered copper foil, household cement, eye pins, self-adhesive black felt, small pin backs, ribbon for bow, small button for bow center, jump ring, and a teapot or bird charm.

1. For each pin, use glass cutter and follow the manufacturer's instructions to cut two same-size pieces from microscope slides.
2. Draw around one slide onto background paper; cut out just inside drawn lines.
3. Cut a piece of lace to fit on background.
4. Layer background and lace between slide pieces; wrapping edges to front and back and mitering corners, cover edges of slides with foil (depending on thickness of lace, it might be necessary to overlap two foil strips).
5. For teapot frame pin, draw around frame on felt, then glue two eye pins to back of frame with eyes extending above and below frame; cut out felt and adhere it to back of frame. Glue pin back to frame. Add a ribbon bow with button center to top eye pin, then using a jump ring, add charm to bottom eye pin.
6. For bird frame pin, glue pin back in place, then glue charm to frame.

BISCUIT QUILT

(shown on page 57)

You will need ⁷/₈ yd. of green fabric (A), ¹/₂ yd. of red fabric (B), 1⁵/₈ yds. of beige fabric (C), 2¹/₄ yds. of green/beige plaid fabric (D), 1⁵/₈ yds. of red/beige plaid fabric (E), and 1¹/₄ yds. of red/green plaid fabric (F); extra-loft polyester batting; and template plastic.

Cut each top square 6¹/₄" square and each backing square 6" square. Refer to the quilt diagram (next page) for color order and use a ⁵/₈" seam allowance for all sewing. You will have raw-edged seams on front side of quilt.

1. Cut twelve top squares and twelve backing squares from fabric A. Cut six top squares and six backing squares from fabric B. Cut 24 top squares and 24 backing squares from fabrics C and E. Cut 34 top squares and 34 backing squares from fabric D. Cut seventeen front squares and seventeen backing squares from fabric F. Cut 117, 4¹/₄" squares from batting.

2. Trace quilting template from page 164 onto template plastic; cut out. Referring to Fig. 1, arrange and mark quilting lines on wrong side of each backing square.

Fig. 1

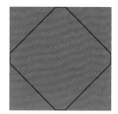

3. For each backing square, center a batting square on wrong side of backing square. Sew along each quilting line to secure batting in place (Fig. 2).

Fig. 2

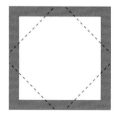

4. For each block, make a small pleat at center of each edge as you pin a matching front square to batting side of a backing square; sew along each edge to secure.
5. Matching back sides, sew blocks together into rows. Sew rows together to assemble quilt. Sew over stitching along outer edges of quilt.
6. Spacing clips about ²/₈" apart and being careful not to clip through stitching, make clips in seams. Shake quilt outside, then wash. Shake outside again and dry (check lint trap several times during drying).

Quilt Diagram

A	D		D	A	D		D	A
D	C	E	C	D	C	E	C	D
	E	B	E		E	B	E	
D	C	E	C	D	C	E	C	D
A	D		D	A	D		D	A
D	C	E	C	D	C	E	C	D
	E	B	E		E	B	E	
D	C	E	C	D	C	E	C	D
A	D		D	A	D		D	A
D	C	E	C	D	C	E	C	D
	E	B	E		E	B	E	
D	C	E	C	D	C	E	C	D
A	D		D	A	D		D	A

WATCH FOB

(shown on page 58)

You will need two crimp beads, jump rings, .015" dia. tiger tail wire, wire cutters, needle-nose pliers, assorted beads, watch face, lobster clasp, and charms.

1. Thread one crimp bead, then a jump ring onto one end of an 8" length of wire. Thread wire end back through crimp bead, and use pliers to crimp to secure.
2. Thread approximately 3" of beads onto wire, then thread wire through bottom of watch; thread wire back through approximately 1" of beads, then add approximately 2" of beads.
3. Thread remaining crimp bead, then lobster clasp onto wire; thread wire back through crimp bead and two or three beads, then crimp to secure. Trim excess wire.
4. Attach a jump ring and charms on opposite side of watch.

MARABOU-TRIMMED PURSE

(shown on page 59)

You will need poster board, ¼ yd. of fabric, spray adhesive, hot glue gun, tracing paper, ½"w decorative trim, 15" length of marabou boa, two shank buttons, and an elastic ponytail holder.

1. Enlarge purse patterns, page 180, 154%; cut out.
2. Using patterns, cut one purse shape from poster board; cut two purse shapes and two gusset shapes from fabric.
3. Apply spray adhesive to one side of poster board piece. Matching edges, smooth one fabric piece over poster board piece. Repeat with remaining fabric piece on opposite side of poster board piece. Fold covered poster board piece as indicated on pattern.
4. For each gusset, press curved edge ¼" to wrong side; press ¼" to wrong side again; top stitch in place.
5. Matching raw edges, refer to Fig. 1 to glue the side and bottom edges of gusset to the side and bottom edges of the purse.

Fig. 1

6. Glue trim along edges of purse, covering raw edges.
7. For handle, glue boa ends to inside top of purse flap.
8. Sew buttons to purse. Fold ponytail holder in half, wrap fold around button, then run one loop through the other loop and pull tight. Stretch ponytail holder over button on flap to secure.

GIFT BOX ORNAMENTS

(shown on page 61)

For each box, you will need primer, spray paint, small papier-mâché box with lid, ribbon at least the width of the box lid, craft glue, pinking sheers, decorative trim, eyelets and eyelet setter, three split rings, 6" length of necklace chain, Beaded Dangle(s) (page 121), and a lobster clasp.

Use craft glue to adhere ribbons and trims to box. If necessary, use clothespins to hold items in place until dry.

1. Prime, then paint entire box and lid.
2. Wrapping excess ribbon to sides of box or lid, cover bottom of box and top of lid with ribbon; trim any excess with pinking sheers.
3. Adhere a piece of ribbon around box starting just below lid.
4. Adhere trim to lid as desired.
5. Following manufacturer's instructions, attach an eyelet in center top of lid and center bottom of box.
6. Attach one split ring ⅝" from one end of chain, then catching ring on inside of box, run chain through eyelet in bottom of box; attach second split ring to last link in chain. Add Beaded Dangle(s) to bottom ring.
7. Run remaining end of chain through eyelet in top of lid, then attach another split ring to last link in chain and lobster clasp to split ring.

FASHION SCARF

(shown on page 58)

Refer to Crochet Basics, page 186, before beginning project.

Finished Size: 5¹/₂" x 62"
(14 cm x 157.5 cm)

Materials:
Bulky Weight Yarn:
7¹/₂ ounces, 340 yards
(210 grams, 311 meters)
Medium Weight Novelty
"Eyelash" Yarn:
1¹/₂ ounces, 50 yards
(40 grams, 45.5 meters)
Crochet hook, size K (6.5 mm) **or**
size needed for gauge

We Used:
Lion Brand® Jiffy® #114 Tree Red
Lion Brand® Fun Fur #113 Red

Gauge: 12 sts and 7 rows =
5¹/₂" (14 cm) square

Gauge Swatch:
5¹/₂" (14 cm) square
Work same as Scarf for 7 rows.

Note: Scarf is crocheted holding two strands of yarn together throughout.

SCARF

Holding one strand of bulky yarn and one strand of novelty yarn together, ch 14.

Row 1 (Right side): Dc in fourth ch from hook (**3 skipped chs count as first dc**) and in each ch across: 12 dc.

Note: Loop a short piece of contrasting color yarn around any stitch to mark Row 1 as **right** side.

Rows 2-4: Ch 3 (counts as **first dc, now and throughout**), turn; dc in next dc and in each dc across.

Row 5: Cut novelty yarn and pick up a second strand of bulky yarn, ch 3, turn; dc in next dc and in each dc across.

Rows 6-8: Ch 3, turn; dc in next dc and in each dc across.

Row 9: Drop one strand of bulky yarn and pick up one strand of novelty yarn, ch 3, turn; dc in next dc and in each dc across.

Row 10: Ch 3, turn; dc in next dc and in each dc across.

Row 11: Cut novelty yarn and pick up a second strand of bulky yarn, ch 3, turn; dc in next dc and in each dc across.

Rows 12-14: Ch 3, turn; dc in next dc and in each dc across.

Row 15: Drop one strand of bulky yarn and pick up one strand of novelty yarn, ch 3, turn; dc in next dc and in each dc across.

Row 16: Ch 3, turn; dc in next dc and in each dc across.

Row 17: Cut novelty yarn and pick up a second strand of bulky yarn, ch 3, turn; dc in next dc and in each dc across.

Repeat Row 16 until Scarf measures approximately 49¹/₂" (125.5 cm) from beginning ch, ending by working a **wrong** side row.

Repeat Rows 9-17, then repeat Rows 6-9. Repeat Row 10, 3 times.

Finish off.

DRAGONFLY NECKLACE

(shown on page 60)

You will need a crimp bead; 6mm silver beads; 24-gauge wire; round-nose jewelry pliers (to bend wire); 4mm green bugle beads, and 4mm green E beads for dragonfly; no-stretch nylon beading string and beading needle; toggle closure; assorted green beads for necklace; and jewelry glue.

Dragonfly Charm
1. Thread crimp bead, then nine silver beads onto one end of wire. Loop remaining end of wire around itself forming a loop, then run wire back through three silver beads.
2. Alternating bugle, then E beads, thread fifteen beads onto wire for first wing. Run end of wire back through the third silver bead to secure.
3. Repeat Step 2 for remaining three wings, crossing wire through third silver bead to make wings above and below bead.
4. Run end of wire back through silver beads and crimp bead, then crimp to secure. Trim excess wire.

Necklace
1. Knot a 24" length of beading string to one end of closure; use a dot of glue to secure knot. Thread approximately 10" of assorted beads onto string.
2. Thread charm onto string, then run string back through last two beads.
3. Thread approximately 10" of assorted beads onto string, then knot string to remaining piece of closure. Trim string ends.

BEAD FRINGED BAG

(shown on page 60)

You will need 4" x 29" piece of fabric for top panel piece (we used a red paisley fabric), 8" x 29" piece of fabric for center panel piece (we used a khaki tone-on-tone fabric), 6" x 29" piece of fabric for bottom panel (we used a rusty-red chenille fabric), 16" x 29" piece of fabric for lining (same fabric as bottom panel), two 3" x 21" pieces of fabric for shoulder straps (same fabric as lining), 1 yd. of beaded bullion fringe, 1 yd. of wooden beaded fringe, 1 yd. of cording, and 1 yd. of beaded cording.

Use a ¹/₂" seam allowance for all sewing.

1. For bag, matching flange to right side of center fabric piece, sew bullion fringe to fabric, then beaded fringe over bullion fringe.
2. Matching right sides and long edges, sew bottom fabric piece to center fabric piece, then top fabric piece to center fabric piece.
3. Hand stitch cording along seam of top and center pieces, just above trims.
4. Matching right sides, sew piece together along short edges, then sew across bottom.
5. To make a flat bottom bag, refer to Fig. 1, fold seam to sides, then stitch across the point; turn bag right side out.

Fig. 1

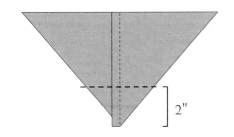

2"

6. For bag lining, matching right sides, sew lining piece together along short edges, leaving an opening for turning at center of seam; sew across bottom. Referring to Fig. 1, fold bottom seam to sides, then stitch across the point. Do not turn right side out.
7. For each handle, match right sides and fold strip in half lengthwise. Sew long edges together; turn right side out. With seam at side, press handle. Top stitch along each side edge of handle.
8. Matching flange to top edge on right side of top fabric piece on bag, pin beaded cording to fabric.
9. For each handle, match raw edges and pin ends of handle to right side of top fabric piece. Baste trim and handles in place; remove pins.
10. Matching top of lining with top of bag and matching side seams, place bag in lining; pin in place (handles will be between bag and lining). Sew pieces together along top edge.
11. Turn bag right side out; sew opening closed.

LOTION BARS AND GIFT BOXES

(shown on page 61)

Lotion Bars

You will need 2 oz. of cocoa butter, 2 oz. of beeswax, 2 oz. of sunflower oil, soap-making molds (we used a ³/₈" x 1⁷/₈" x 2¹/₂" mold and a 2¹/₄" dia. mold with a raised snowflake), and clear-backed poinsettia stickers.

Mixture will make approximately four lotion bars.

1. Melt cocoa butter and beeswax in the microwave in one minute increments until completely melted. Stir in sunflower oil.
2. Pour mixture into molds and allow to cool completely.
3. Remove bars from molds and adhere stickers to flat bars.

Snowflake Box

You will need small gift box (ours measures 2³/₄" x 2¹/₄" x 1" and has a cut out opening in top with a flap that covers opening), spray adhesive, decorative paper, craft glue, hole punch, elastic ponytail holder, shank button, and snowflake charms with hangers removed (if applicable).

1. Carefully disassemble and flatten box. Apply spray adhesive to outside of box. Place box on decorative paper; cut out. Glue box back together, then place Lotion Bars in box before closing.
2. For closure, punch hole in lid of box. Making a knot at one end of ponytail holder loop, thread loop through hole in lid, catching knot on inside. Sew button to front of box for loop to slip over.
3. Glue snowflake charms to top of box.

Poinsettia Box

You will need a gold ink pad, small gift box (ours measures 2³/₄" x 2¹/₄" x 1" and has a cut out opening in top with a flap that covers opening), embossing powder, heating tool, ribbon, and clear-backed poinsettia stickers.

1. Stamp box with ink pad; sprinkle embossing powder on wet ink, then follow manufacturer's instructions to emboss box. Continue stamping and embossing until desired effect is achieved.
2. For closure, run a length of ribbon though holes in box, and tie them into a bow.
3. Adhere sticker to top of box.

STORY TIME TAPE SET

(shown on page 59)

You will need white spray primer; 9⅝" x 7" x 2⅜" papier-mâché book-shaped box; craft glue; red corduroy; red plaid, red velvet, and white papers; 2"w white flocked, ⅝"w green, and ⅝"w red ribbons; tracing paper; fusible interfacing; ⅜" dia. snap; four eyelets and eyelet setter; cassette tape (with favorite story recorded on it) and case; red card stock for cassette tape insert; red chenille trim; and child's favorite book that fits inside box.

Use craft glue to adhere fabric, papers, and ribbon to box. If necessary, use clothespins to hold items in place until dry.

1. Apply primer to entire box.
2. Line bottom inside area of box with corduroy.
3. Wrapping excess to inside, cover front and back of book with plaid paper; trim excess as needed.
4. Wrapping excess to inside and extending edges to front and back of book, cover spine with velvet paper.
5. Trimming curves to fit, cover "pages" with white ribbon.
6. Fuse a 6" x 9" piece of interfacing to an 6" x 9" piece of corduroy. Trace pocket pattern, page 175, onto tracing paper; cut out. Using pattern, cut pocket from fused corduroy. Glue a length of green ribbon along top inner and outer edges of pocket. Attach one side of snap to center top of pocket.
7. Matching bottom edges, center and glue bottom third of an 8" length of green ribbon to front inside cover of book. Attach remaining side of snap 2½" from top of ribbon; notch top of ribbon.
8. Folding and gluing pocket as indicated on pattern, glue pocket to inside front cover of book.
9. For bow, cut a 6" length of red ribbon. Glue ends together, forming a loop. Wrap and glue a 3" length of ribbon around center of loop. Cut a 6½" length of ribbon for streamer. Glue streamer to book, then glue bow to top of streamer; notch end of streamer.

10. Write or type and print message for front of book on white paper; cut out. Attach eyelets at each corner of paper. Glue message to front of book.
11. For tape case, use cassette insert as a pattern to cut a piece of card stock to fit inside case. Write or type and print message for front of tape case on white paper; cut out. Glue message to card stock, then glue trim around message, tying into a bow at bottom (Fig. 1).

Fig. 1

12. Place cassette tape in pocket and snap shut. Include favorite storybook inside box.

Great Goodies to Give

SOUP MIX JAR
(shown on page 64)

You will need raffia, jar with lid, hot glue gun, basil leaves, pepperberry clusters, poster board, decorative papers, craft glue stick, brass paper fastener, and a small cargo tag.

Use the craft glue stick for all gluing unless otherwise indicated.

1. Tie several lengths of raffia around the jar, then hot glue a bay leaf behind the knot and pepperberries over the knot.
2. For lid cover, cut a piece of poster board and paper to fit the top of the lid; glue the paper to the poster board. Attach the fastener at one corner of the cover and hot glue the cover to the lid.
3. Glue a small piece of paper to the cargo tag, then trim the paper edges to match. Tear, then glue a small piece of paper to the tag, then hot glue a knot of raffia, a bay leaf, and pepperberries to the tag. Write message on back of tag, then wrap the tag ties around the fastener.

SALAD DRESSING GIFT SET
(shown on page 65)

You will need two canning jars (each with lids and rings), red and green decorative papers, craft glue, $5/8$"w red ribbon, round metal-rimmed tags, artificial stems of small leaves with berries, fine-point black marker, silver spray paint for metal, salad dressings, basket, and wood excelsior.

1. For each jar, measure around the jar, then add $1/2$"; cut a strip of red paper $2 1/2$"w by the determined measurement. Cut a strip of green paper $2 1/4$"w by the determined measurement.
2. Overlapping at back, layer and glue the red, then green paper around the jar.
3. Overlapping at front, drape a length of ribbon around the jar; glue it in place.
4. Glue a piece of green paper to tag. Use marker to write message on tag; glue tag to jar. Glue a few leaves and berries behind the tag.
5. Paint the outside of the jar ring silver.
6. Draw around jar lid on green paper; cut out just inside drawn line. Use marker to write dressing name on paper piece.
7. Add the lid, decorative paper, and ring to each jar.
8. Fill the basket with excelsior, then place the jars in the basket. Decorate the basket with berry stems.

BAY LEAF WREATH BOX
(shown on page 66)

You will need découpage glue, round papier-mâché box with lid, brown paper bags, tacky glue, dried bay leaves, raffia, red corrugated craft paper, and a self-adhesive foam spacer.

Use tacky glue for all gluing, unless otherwise indicated.

1. Follow *Découpaging*, page 185, to glue, cover the outside of the box and lid with torn pieces of brown paper.
2. Glue a ''wreath'' of bay leaves to the box lid.
3. Tie several lengths of raffia into a bow, then glue it to the top of the wreath.
4. For the gift tag, write your message on a small piece of torn brown paper, then glue it and a small bay leaf to a piece of red paper. Use the spacer to attach the tag just under the bow.

PAINTED JAR

(shown on page 67)

You will need 1"w painter's masking tape, glass jar with lid, light blue permanent enamel paint, paintbrush, white paint pen, découpage glue, ultra-fine light blue glitter and round iridescent glitter for snowflake centers, and white sheer ribbon.

1. Tape off a 1"w stripe around the jar, then paint the stripe and the lid blue; allow to dry. Remove the tape.
2. Using the paint pen, draw snowflakes and dots around the jar and on the lid; allow to dry.
3. Apply découpage glue to the painted areas, then while still wet, add glitter; shake off excess and allow to dry.
4. Using a length of ribbon to secure loops and to attach bow to jar, follow the instructions for *Bows*, page 152, to make a Multi-Loop Bow.

FABRIC-COVERED CHEST

(shown on page 67)

You will need a 4¹/₄"h x 6¹/₂"l x 4¹/₄"d papier-mâché hinged chest with clasp, craft glue, fabric, metallic gold wrapping paper, small hangtag, card stock, ¹/₈" dia. hole punch, ¹/₈" dia. eyelet and eyelet setter, opaque gold paint pen, 2¹/₂"w wire-edged ribbon, and thin gold cording.

1. Remove clasp from chest.
2. Measure length of chest and add ¹/₂"; referring to Fig. 1, measure around chest and add 1". Cut a piece of fabric the determined measurements.

Fig. 1

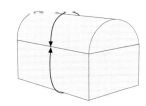

3. Draw around ends of chest onto fabric; cut out shape ¹/₄" outside the drawn lines.
4. Center and glue end pieces to ends of chest; clip corners and glue edges of fabric to chest. Use a craft knife to cut fabric for opening (Fig. 2).

Fig. 2

5. Press long edges of remaining fabric piece under ¹/₄", then center and glue fabric piece around chest; glue ends to inside of chest.
6. Line inside of chest with wrapping paper.
7. Reattach clasp to chest.
8. For gift tag, glue hangtag to card stock; cut out ¹/₈" outside tag. Punch a hole in tag, then attach eyelet. Paint dots on tag.
9. Tie ribbon into a bow around chest, then thread cording through knot in bow. Hang gift tag from cording.

CANDY CANE GIFT SACKS

(shown on page 69)

For each sack, you will need red or green and cream card stock, decorative-edge craft scissors, alphabet rubber stamps and an ink pad, craft glue stick, red or green lunch-size paper sack, hole punch, red or green raffia, hot glue gun, artificial holly leaves, and a candy cane.

1. For card, cut a 5¹/₂" x 6" piece of red or green card stock; fold in half widthwise. For tag, use craft scissors to cut a piece of cream card stock slightly smaller than the card front.
2. Draw a dashed and dotted border along edges of tag, then stamp it with "SNACK MIX" and "TO" and "FROM." Write names on the tag.
3. Use the glue stick to adhere the tag to the card front.
4. Fold the top of the sack over 1". Place the card over the top of the sack, then punching through all layers, punch two holes at the top center of the sack. Thread a length of raffia through the holes, and tie it into a bow at the front of the sack.
5. Hot glue holly leaves and candy cane to the front of the sack.

HAND-PAINTED BOWL

(shown on page 68

You will need a pasta bowl, rubbing alcohol, tracing paper, transfer paper and a stylus, assorted colors of glass paint, and paintbrushes.

Follow manufacturer's instructions for applying and curing paint; allow to dry after each application. Refer to color key while painting project. Project is intended for decorative purposes only.

1. Clean bowl with alcohol.
2. Divide bowl rim into approx. 2"w equal sections based on outer rim measurement.
3. Trace chef and tomato outline patterns from page 183 onto tracing paper. Transfer patterns to rim of pasta bowl.
4. Draw large and small checkerboard patterns and stripe patterns on remaining sections of bowl.
5. Paint black background around chef and tomato patterns.

6. Referring to photos 1a and 1b, paint basecoats on chef and tomato sections; paint basecoats on remaining sections.

Photo 1a

Photo 1b

7. Referring to photos 2a and 2b, shade chef and tomato sections; shade remaining sections.

Photo 2a

Photo 2b

8. Tranfer detail pattern from page 183 onto chef and tomato sections. Referring to photos 3a and 3b, paint details on chef and paint stems and leaves on tomatoes; add detail lines to remaining sections.

Photo 3a

Photo 3b

STANDING SANTA BAG
(shown on page 70)

You will need tracing paper; white, red, cream, green, gold, brown, and black felt; pinking sheers; polyester fiberfill; fabric glue; three red buttons; and hook and loop fasteners.

1. Enlarge body pattern, page 181, 142%; cut out. Trace beard, hat, star, and tree patterns, pages 181 and 182, onto tracing paper; cut out.
2. Use patterns to cut one beard from white felt, two bodies from red felt, one face from cream felt, three trees and one hat from green felt, and four stars from gold felt.
3. For tree trunks, cut three strips from brown felt. For snow bank, cut a 7¹/₂" x 8" piece from white felt, then cut curves along one long edge. Using pinking sheers, cut a ³/₄" x 3" strip for mustache from white felt.
4. Leaving the bottom open for stuffing and using a ¹/₄" seam allowance, layer the body pieces, then the face piece, and sew pieces together; trim close to seam. Stuff head with fiberfill.
5. For hat, overlap and glue long edges together. Fold up one end of hat ¹/₂" for cuff. Glue hat to head. Wrap a piece of thread around the tip of the hat, then glue a star over the thread. Glue three buttons to the cuff of the hat.
6. Leaving a ³/₄"w band intact at top of beard for gluing, cut ¹/₂"w strips in felt; glue to head.
7. For mustache, wrap a piece of thread around the center of the mustache, then glue a red square of felt for the nose over the string; glue the mustache to the top center of the beard.
8. For eyes, cut two pieces of black felt; glue in place.

9. Glue 2" of the snow bank to the front bottom of the body.
10. Position and glue the tree trunks, trees, and stars to the body.
11. With bag facing down, fold corners of snow bank 1¹/₂" towards center; glue in place. Align and adhere hook and loop fasteners to the snow bank and the back of the bag.

DECORATED TIN
(shown on page 72)

You will need white kraft paper, large coffee tin with lid, spray adhesive, decorative-edge craft scissors, Christmas cards, decorative paper, craft glue stick, Christmas stickers, drawing compass, yellow card stock, and thin ribbon.

1. Cut a piece of white paper to fit around the tin with a 1" overlap. Use spray adhesive to attach the paper to the tin.
2. Using craft scissors, cut messages and images from Christmas cards, then cut larger background pieces from decorative paper for "frames." Glue the messages and images to the "frames", then glue them around the tin. Add stickers.
3. Use the compass to draw a circle for the center and an outer ring on decorative paper to fit the lid; cut out. Glue the papers to the lid.
4. Photocopy the verse pattern, page 183, on yellow paper; cut out. Center and glue the verse to the lid. Add stickers to the lid.
5. Glue a length of ribbon around the lid and along the bottom of the tin.

GRANOLA BAR WRAPPER
(shown on page 73)

You will need color pencils, craft glue stick, and a green foil-wrapped granola bar.

1. Photocopy the wrapper design, page 183; cut out.
2. Use color pencils to color the design.
3. Overlapping at back, glue the wrapper around the granola bar.

GIFT TAG ORNAMENT
(shown on page 73)

You will need assorted decorative papers, decorative-edge craft scissors, craft glue stick, cargo tag, hole punch, acrylic paint, paintbrushes, unfinished wooden beads, hot glue gun, red chenille yarn, wood filler, sandpaper, and miniature holly leaves with berries.

1. Cut several pieces of decorative paper with craft scissors, then layer and glue them on the cargo tag. Print a small card using a favorite font on a computer or hand letter a card; cut out. Glue the card to the bottom of the tag. Punch a hole in the decorative paper part of tag.
2. For miniature ornaments, paint the beads to coordinate with the ornaments on the Granola Bar Wrapper, above, then hot glue ends of a length of yarn into the holes in beads for the hanger. Fill the open ends of the beads with wood filler; when dry, sand and touch up with paint.
3. Hot glue the bead's hanger to the tag, then hot glue the holly over the hanger.
4. For the ornament hanger, loop a length of yarn through the hole in the tag.

Patterns

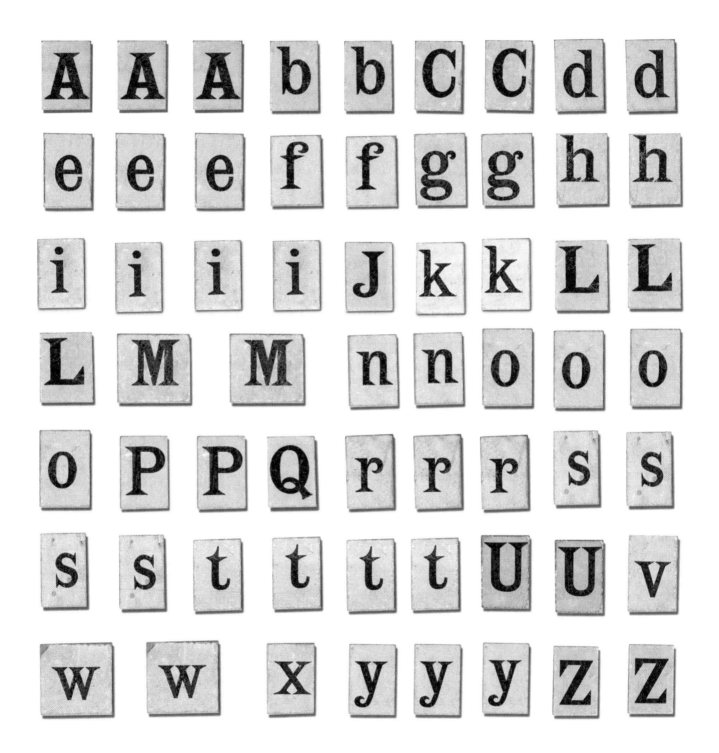

PAPIER-MÂCHÉ ORNAMENTS
(page 141)
AND
FRAMED PIECES
(page 142)

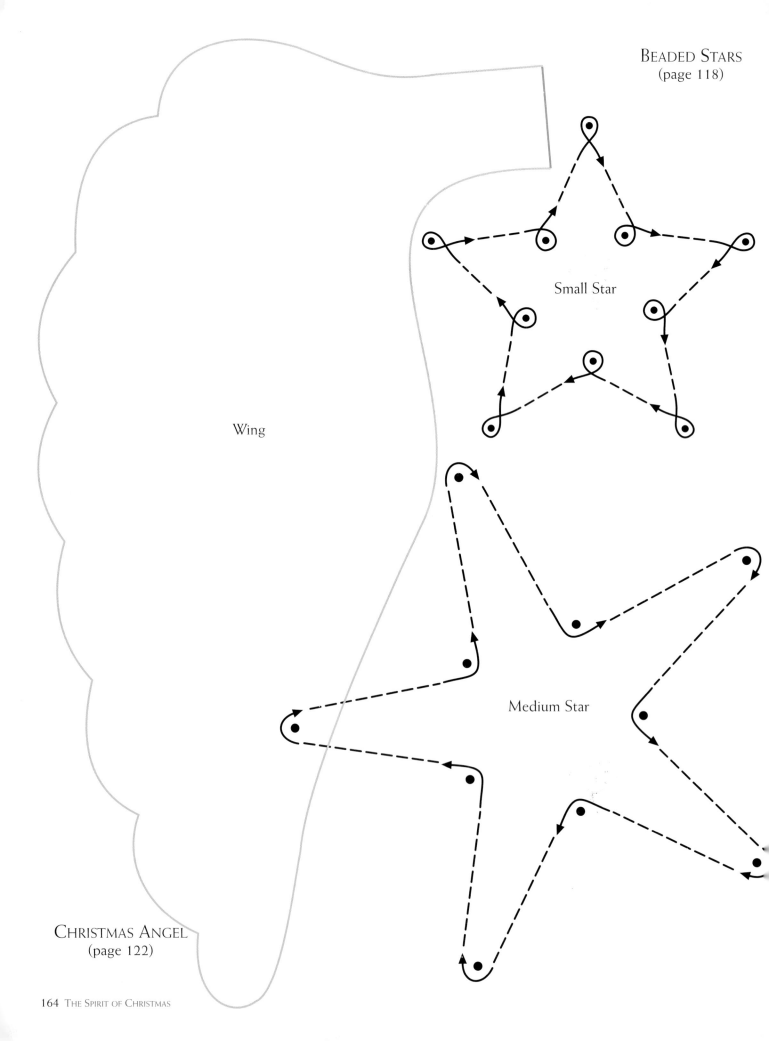

Small Star

Wing

Medium Star

CHRISTMAS ANGEL
(page 122)

Heart

Pom-pom

ORNAMENTS
(page 124)

Hat

Trim

S-HOOK
HANGER
(page 124)

Snowflake

Spiral

Whimsical Foam Stocking
(page 124)

Band

Countdown Santa
(page 126)

Pocket

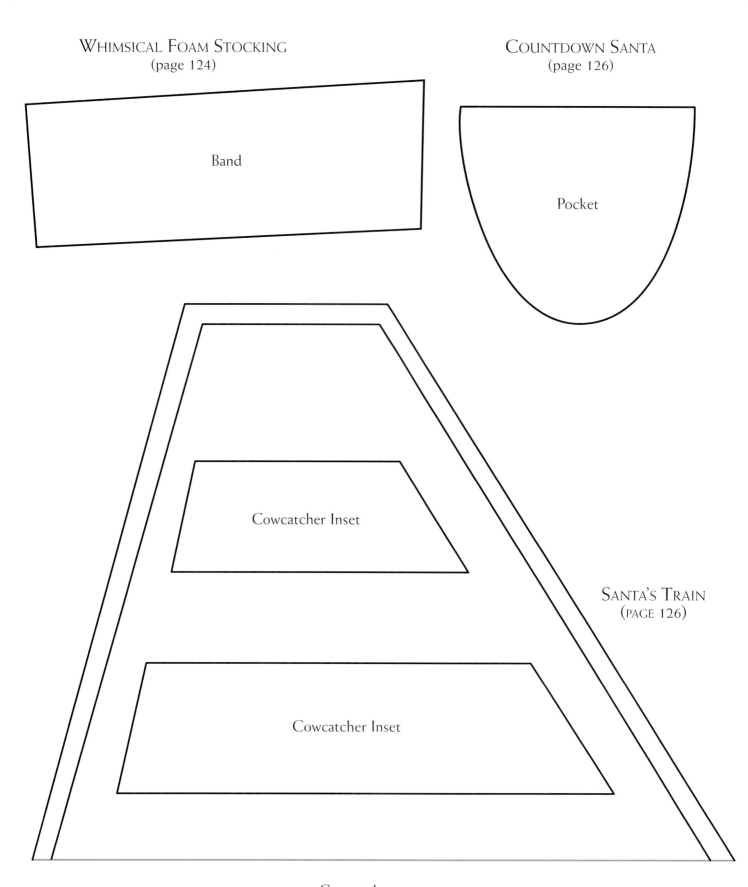

Cowcatcher Inset

Cowcatcher Inset

Santa's Train
(PAGE 126)

Cowcatcher

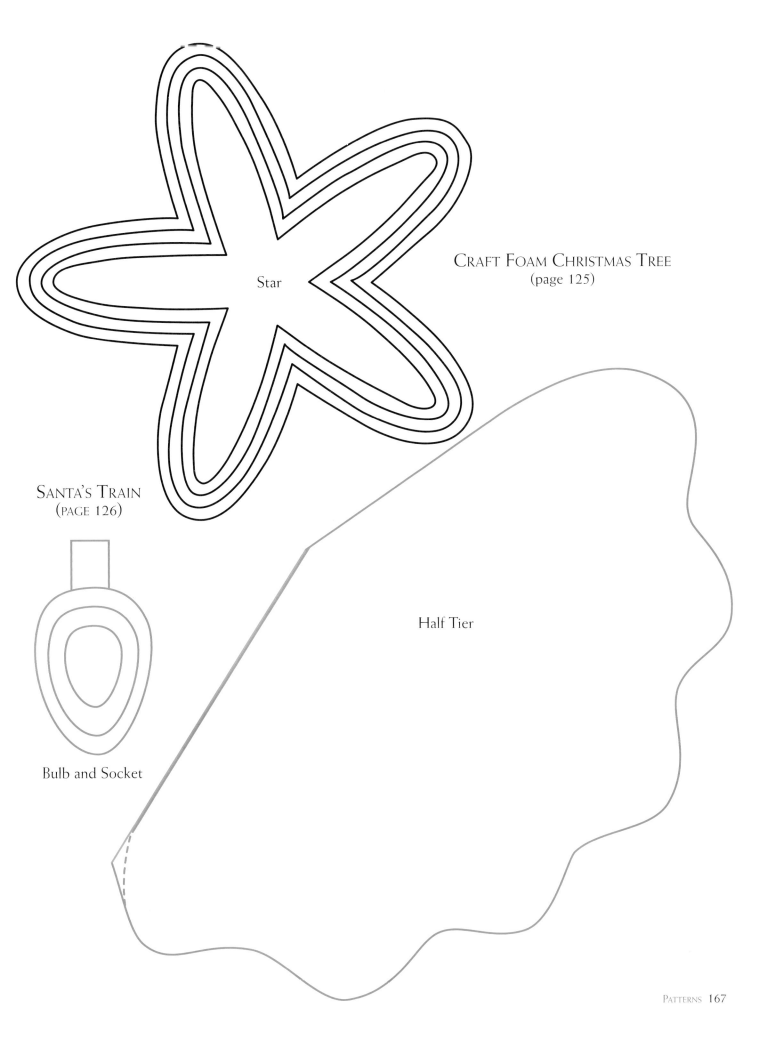

Star

CRAFT FOAM CHRISTMAS TREE
(page 125)

SANTA'S TRAIN
(PAGE 126)

Half Tier

Bulb and Socket

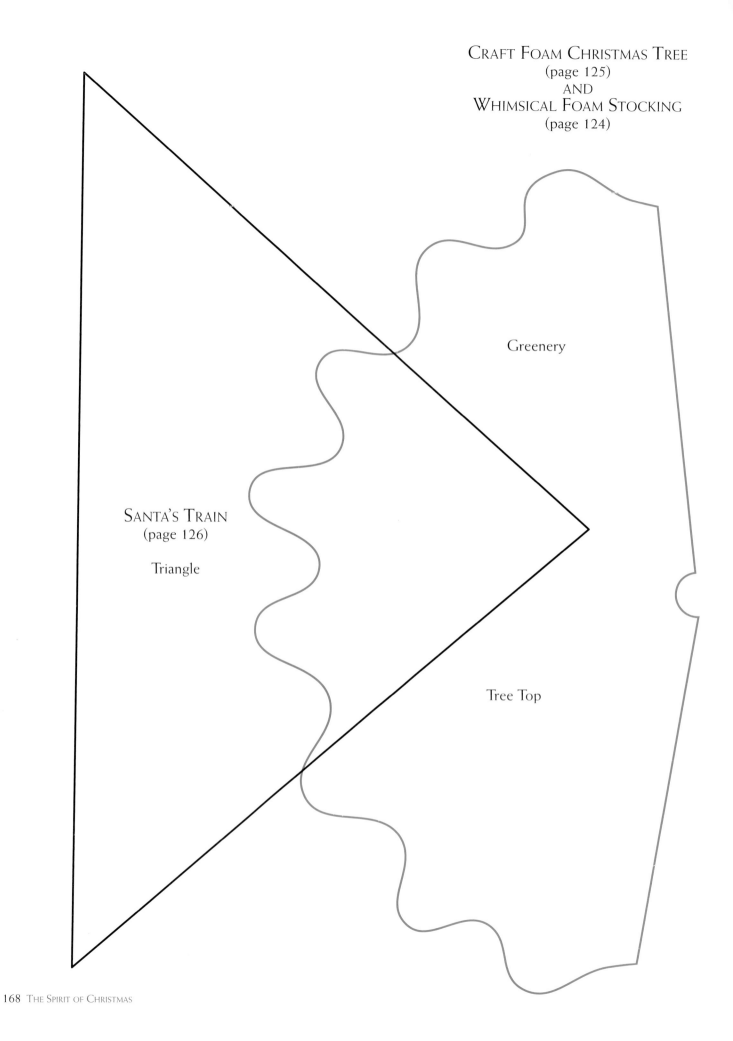

CRAFT FOAM CHRISTMAS TREE
(page 125)
AND
WHIMSICAL FOAM STOCKING
(page 124)

Greenery

SANTA'S TRAIN
(page 126)

Triangle

Tree Top

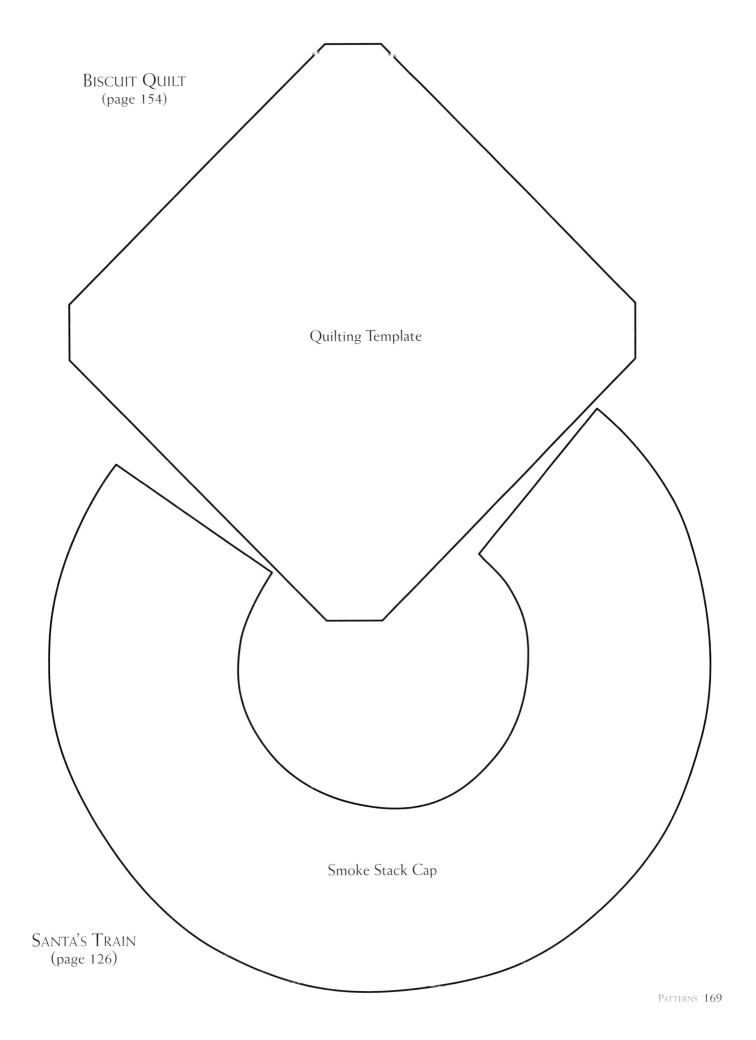

BISCUIT QUILT
(page 154)

Quilting Template

Smoke Stack Cap

SANTA'S TRAIN
(page 126)

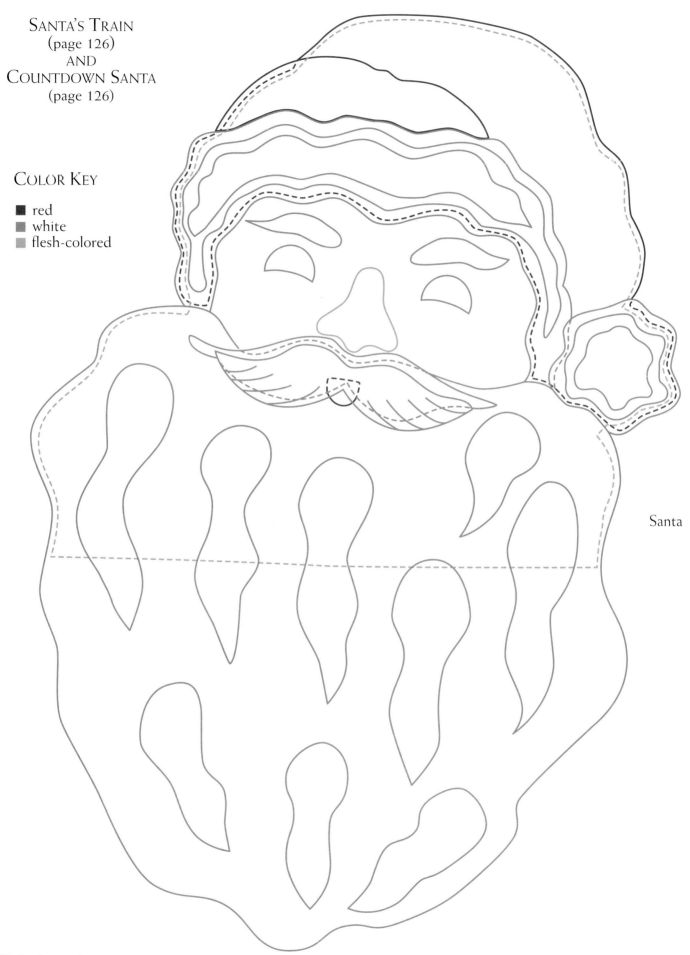

SANTA'S TRAIN
(page 126)
AND
COUNTDOWN SANTA
(page 126)

COLOR KEY

■ red
■ white
■ flesh-colored

Santa

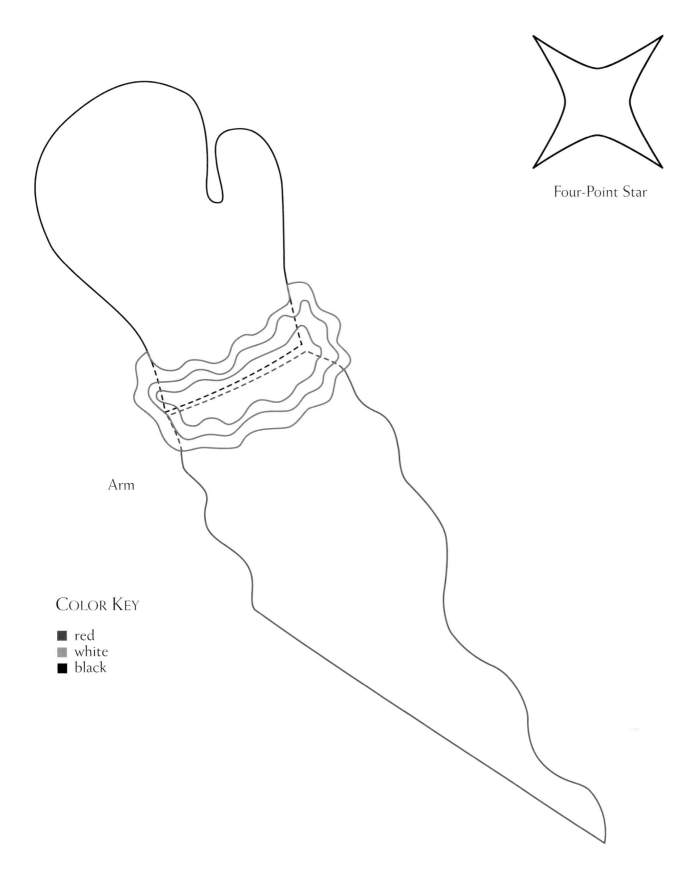

Four-Point Star

Arm

COLOR KEY

▪ red
▪ white
▪ black

ST. NICOLAS PILLOW
(page 136)

SANTA ORNAMENTS
(page 137)

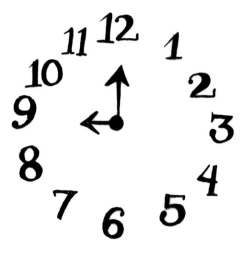

CLOCK ORNAMENTS
(page 138)

SANTA ORNAMENTS
(page 137)

SANTA ORNAMENTS
(page 137)

PLACEMENT DIAGRAM

CROSS-STITCHED SANTAS
(page 136)

CROSS-STITCHED SANTAS
(page 136)

STITCH COUNT (58w x 74h)

14count	4¼"	x	5⅜"
16count	3⅝"	x	4⅝"
18count	3¼"	x	4⅛"
22count	2¾"	x	3⅜"

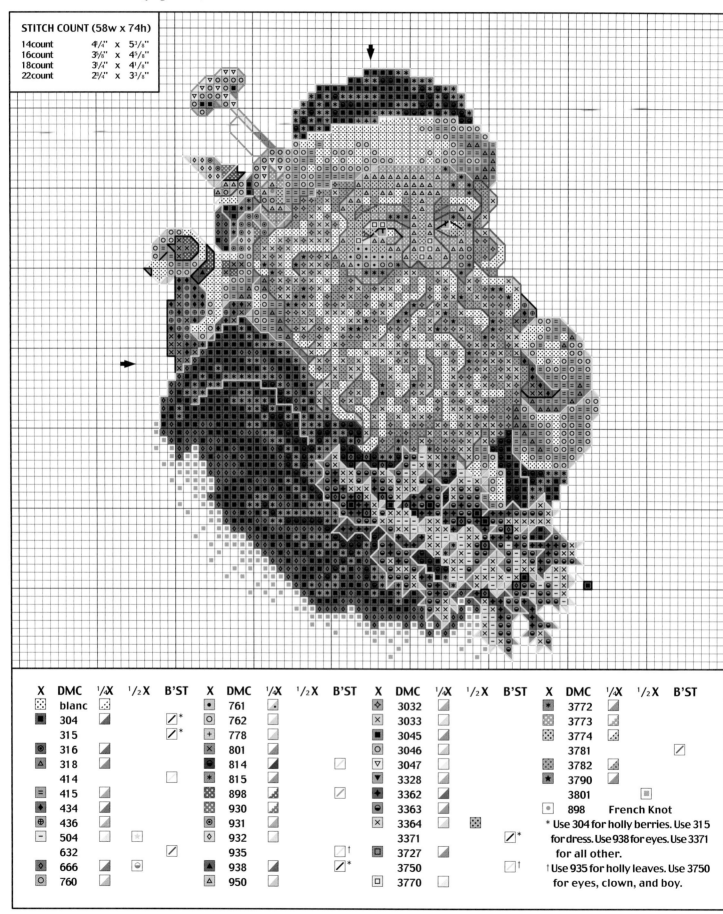

X	DMC	¼X	½X	B'ST	X	DMC	¼X	½X	B'ST	X	DMC	¼X	½X	B'ST	X	DMC	¼X	½X	B'ST
	blanc				•	761					3032				*	3772			
	304			✓*	○	762				×	3033					3773			
	315			✓*	+	778					3045					3774			
⊙	316				×	801				○	3046					3781			✓
△	318					814				▽	3047					3782			
	414				*	815				▼	3328				★	3790			
=	415					898					3362					3801			
◆	434					930					3363				◉	898		French Knot	
⊕	436				◉	931				×	3364								
−	504				◇	932					3371			✓*	* Use 304 for holly berries. Use 315				
	632			✓		935			†		3727				for dress. Use 938 for eyes. Use 3371				
◆	666				▲	938			✓*		3750			†	for all other.				
○	760				△	950					3770				† Use 935 for holly leaves. Use 3750				

* Use 304 for holly berries. Use 315 for dress. Use 938 for eyes. Use 3371 for all other.

† Use 935 for holly leaves. Use 3750 for eyes, clown, and boy.

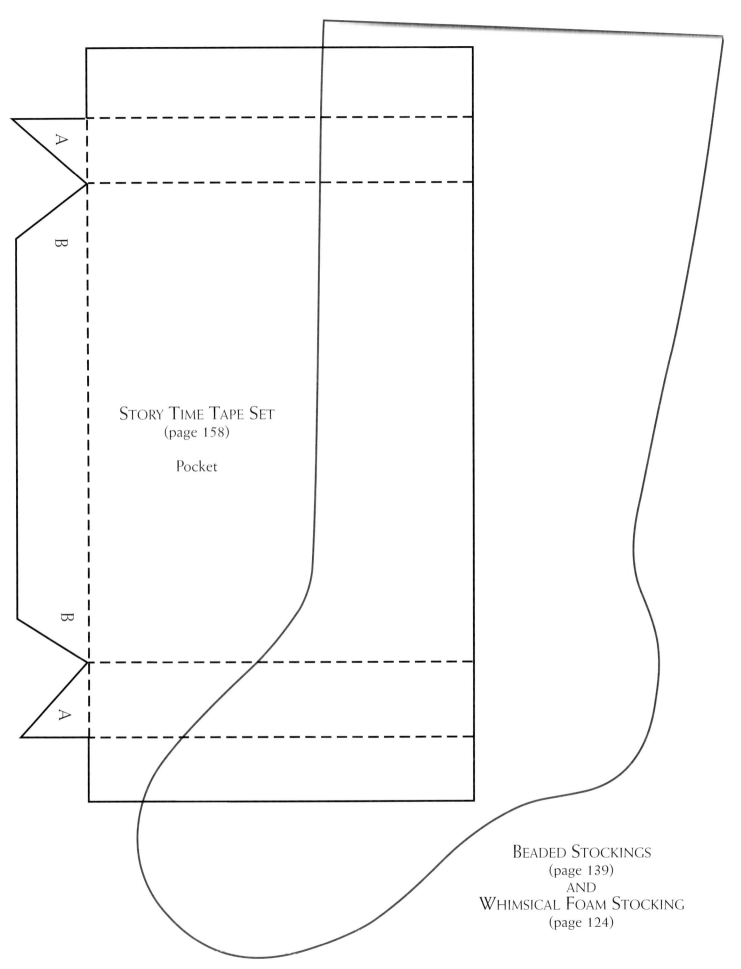

A

B

B

A

STORY TIME TAPE SET
(page 158)

Pocket

BEADED STOCKINGS
(page 139)
AND
WHIMSICAL FOAM STOCKING
(page 124)

STAR TABLE TOPPER
(page 146)

Star Point

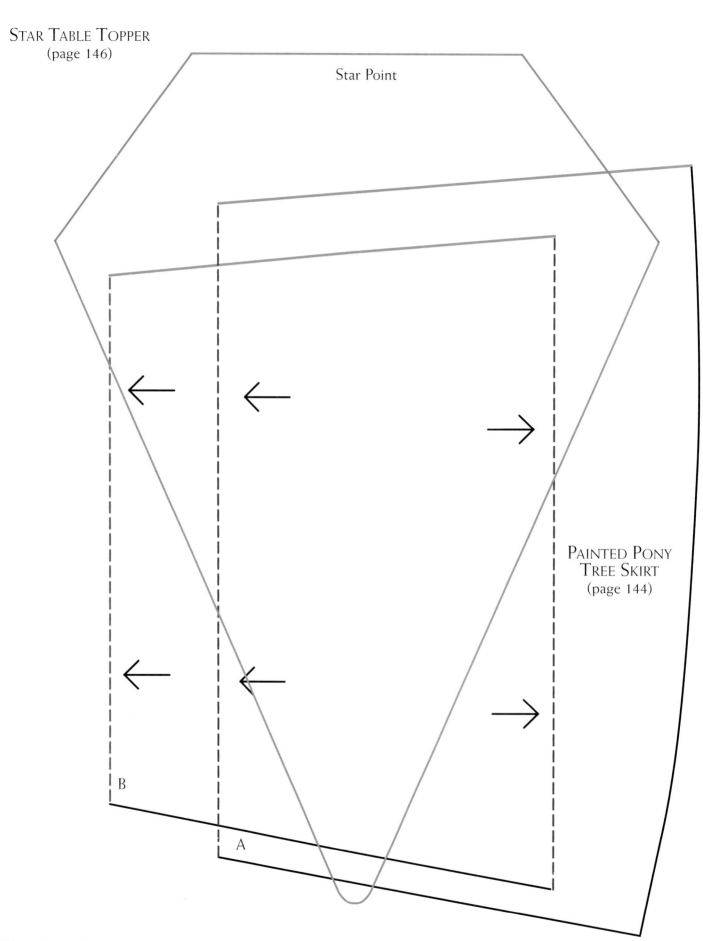

PAINTED PONY
TREE SKIRT
(page 144)

B

A

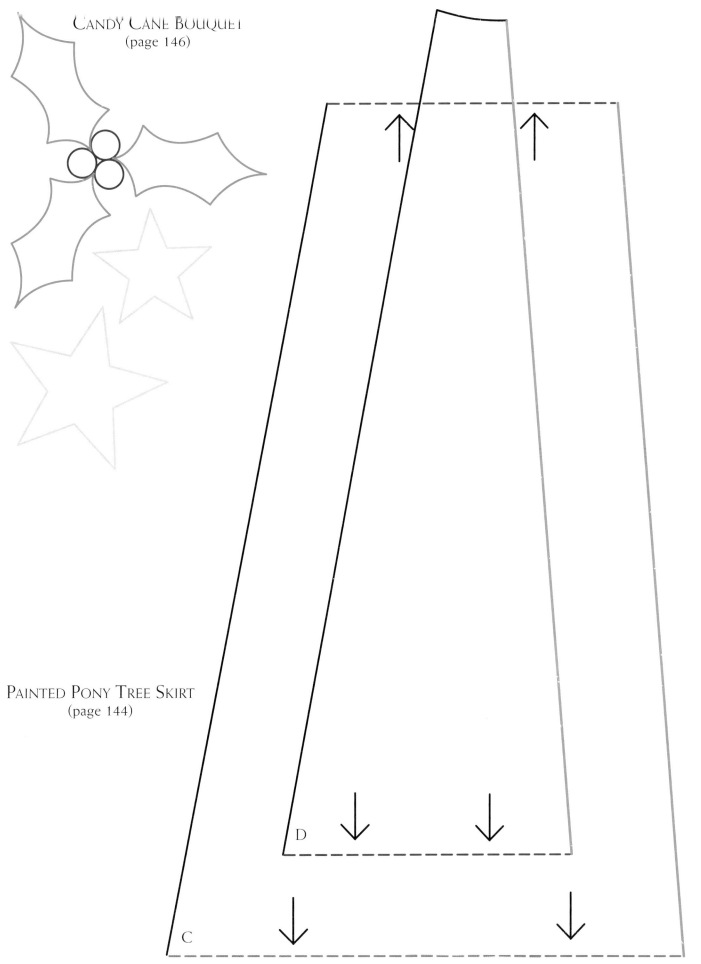

CANDY CANE BOUQUET
(page 146)

PAINTED PONY TREE SKIRT
(page 144)

D

C

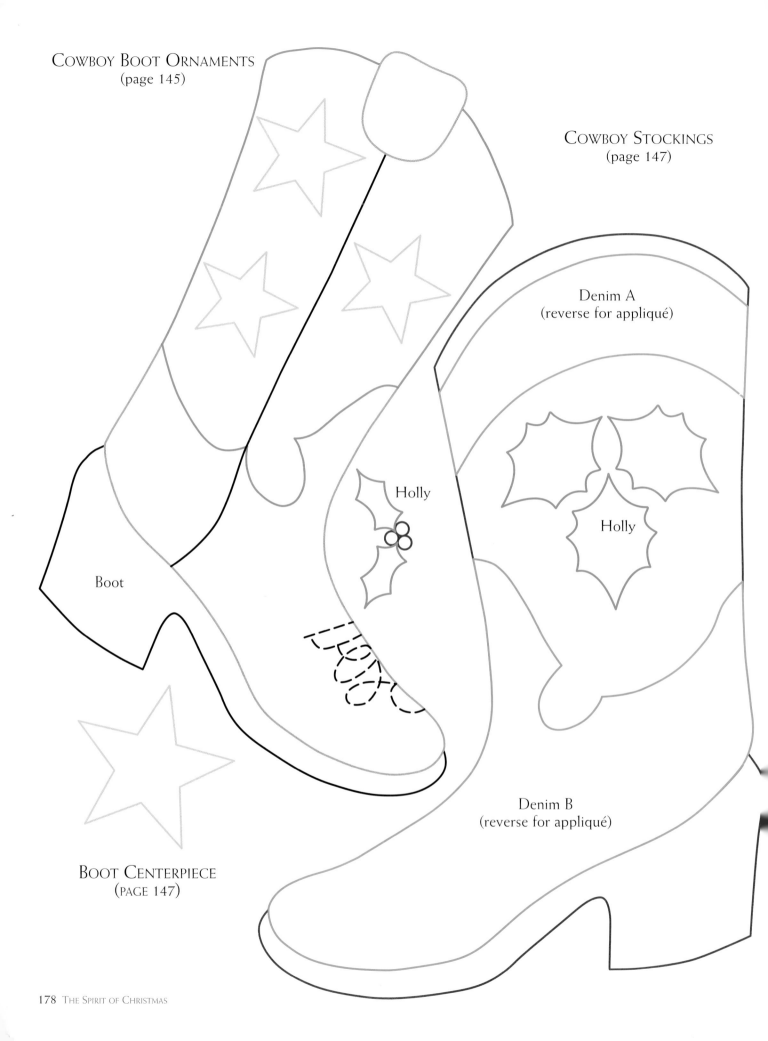

COWBOY BOOT ORNAMENTS
(page 145)

COWBOY STOCKINGS
(page 147)

Denim A
(reverse for appliqué)

Holly

Holly

Boot

Denim B
(reverse for appliqué)

BOOT CENTERPIECE
(PAGE 147)

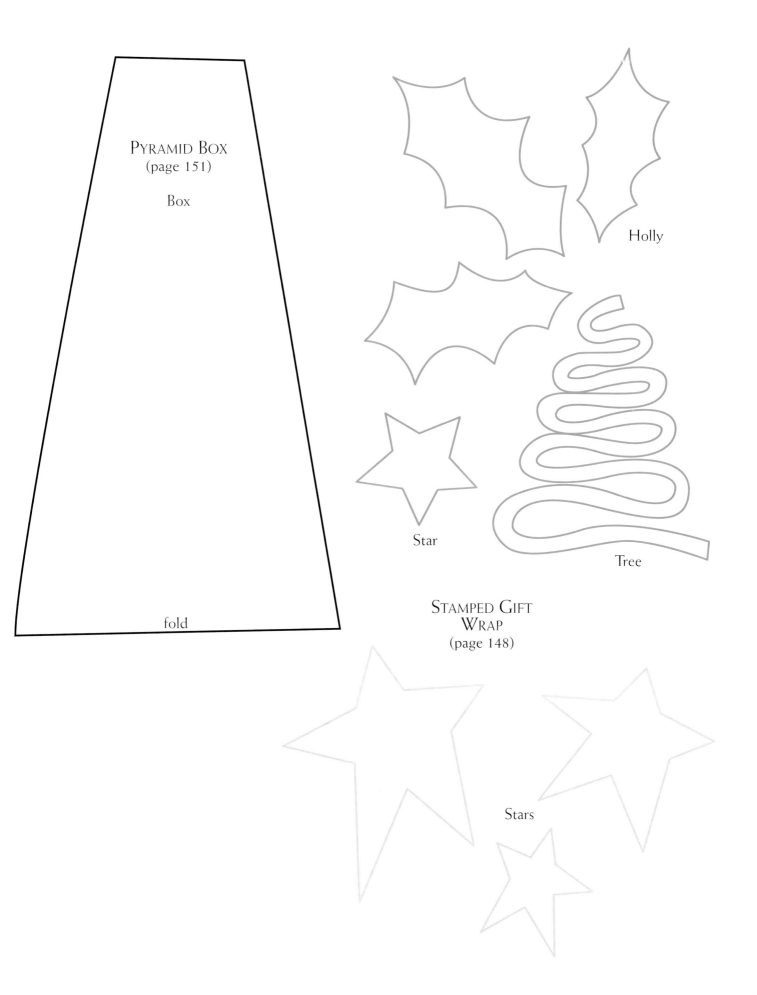

PYRAMID BOX
(page 151)

Box

fold

Holly

Star

Tree

STAMPED GIFT
WRAP
(page 148)

Stars

Gusset

Purse

WRAP IT UP ORGANIZER
(page 149)

Holly Leaf

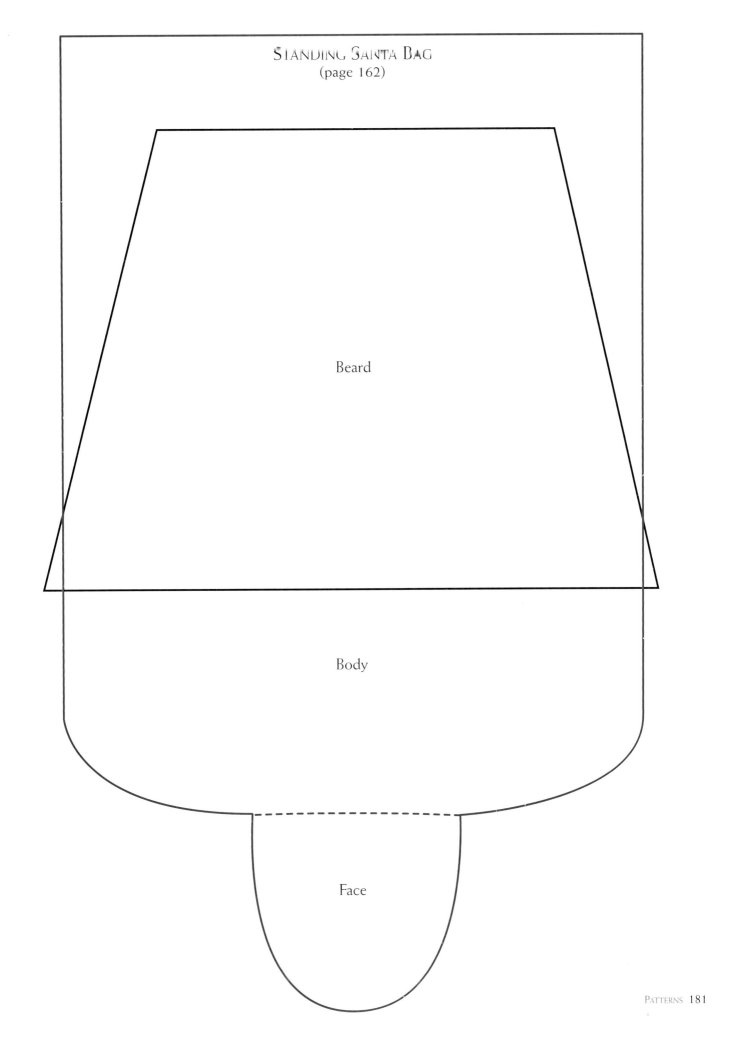

STANDING SANTA BAG
(page 162)

Beard

Body

Face

STANDING SANTA BAG
(page 162)

Hat

Tree

Star

I will honor **Christmas** in my heart and try to keep it all the year.

CHARLES DICKENS

DECORATED TIN
(page 162)

HAND-PAINTED BOWL
(page 161)

Chef Detail

Chef Outline

Tomato Detail

Tomato Outline

Sweets for thee...

A keepsake for the tree!

GRANOLA BAR WRAPPER
(page 162)

General Instructions

MAKING PATTERNS
WHOLE PATTERNS
When the whole pattern is shown, place tracing paper over pattern and trace pattern. For a more durable pattern, use a permanent marker to trace pattern onto stencil plastic.

HALF PATTERNS
When only half of a pattern is shown (indicated by a solid blue line on the pattern), fold tracing paper in half. Place the fold along the blue line and trace pattern half; turn folded paper over and draw over traced lines on remaining side of paper to form a whole pattern.

Or, fold fabric in half. Trace pattern half onto tracing paper and cut out. Place "blue line" of pattern along fold in fabric and pin in place. Cutting through both layers, cut along black line(s) of pattern to cut out a whole pattern.

MULTIPLE-PART PATTERNS
When tracing a multiple-part pattern, match the dashed lines and arrows to trace the patterns onto tracing paper, forming a whole pattern.

STACKED OR OVERLAPPED PATTERNS
When pattern pieces are stacked or overlapped, place tracing paper over pattern and follow a single color to trace pattern. Repeat to trace each pattern separately onto tracing paper.

PAINTING TECHNIQUES
A disposable foam plate makes a good palette for holding a small amount of paint and mixing colors. It can easily be placed in a large resealable plastic bag to keep remaining paint wet while waiting for an area of applied paint to dry.

Always clean brushes thoroughly after painting is complete, to keep them in good condition.

Following the manufacturer's instructions will produce the best results for any paint product. If you are unfamiliar with a specific painting technique, practice on a scrap of wood, cardboard, paper, or fabric before beginning project.

Work in a well-ventilated area and protect work surfaces with newspaper or a drop cloth.

TRANSFERRING PATTERNS
Note: If transferring pattern onto a dark surface, use a light-colored transfer paper to transfer pattern.

Trace pattern onto tracing paper. Using removable tape, tape tracing paper pattern to project. Place transfer paper (or graphite paper), coated side down, between project and tracing paper. Use a stylus or pencil to lightly draw over pattern lines onto project.

PAINTING BASECOATS
A basecoat is a solid color of paint that covers the project's surface. Use a medium to large paintbrush for large areas and a small brush for small areas. Do not overload brush. Allow paint to dry after each coat.

DETAILS/LINE WORK
To prevent smudging lines or ruining your pen, let painted areas dry before adding details/line work.

Use a permanent marker or paint pen to draw over transferred detail lines or to create freehanded details on project.

If painting, mix paint with water to an ink-like consistency. Dip a liner brush into thinned paint. Use tip of brush to outline or create details on project.

SPONGE PAINTING
This technique creates a soft, mottled look on the project's surface.

Practice sponge-painting on scrap paper until desired look is achieved. Try using different sponge types, such as a natural sponge, a cosmetic sponge, and a household sponge, to create different appearances.

1. Dampen sponge with water; squeeze out excess.
2. Dip sponge into paint, then blot on a paper towel to remove excess paint.
3. Use a light stamping motion to paint project. Allow to dry.
4. If using more than one color of paint, repeat Steps 1 – 3, using a new sponge piece for each color.
5. If desired, repeat technique using one color again to soften edges or to lighten a heavy application of one or more paint colors.

SHADING AND HIGHLIGHTING (side loading):
Dip one corner of a flat brush in water; blot on a paper towel. Dip dry corner of brush into paint. Stroke brush back and forth on palette until there is a gradual change from paint to water in each brush stroke. Stroke loaded side of brush along detail line on project, pulling brush toward you and turning project if necessary.

For shading, side load brush with a darker color of paint.

For highlighting, side load brush with lighter color of paint.

SEALING
If a project will be handled frequently or used outdoors, we recommend sealing the item with clear sealer. Sealers are available in spray or brush-on forms and in a variety of finishes. Follow the manufacturer's instructions to apply sealer.

DÉCOUPAGING

1. Cut desired motifs from fabric or paper.
2. Apply découpage glue to wrong sides of motifs.
3. Overlapping as necessary, arrange motifs on project as desired. Smooth in place and allow to dry.
4. Allowing to dry after each application, apply two to three coats of sealer to project.

FUSIBLE APPLIQUÉS

To prevent darker fabrics from showing through, white or light-colored appliqué fabrics may need to be lined with fusible interfacing before applying paper-backed fusible web.

To make reverse appliqué pieces, trace pattern onto tracing paper; turn traced pattern over and continue to follow all steps using the reversed pattern.

1. Use a pencil to trace pattern or draw around reversed pattern onto paper side of web as many times as indicated for a single fabric. Repeat for additional patterns and fabrics.
2. Follow manufacturer's instructions to fuse traced patterns to wrong side of fabrics. Do not remove paper backing.
3. Cut out appliqué pieces along traced lines. Remove paper backing.
4. Arrange appliqués, web side down, on project, overlapping as necessary. Appliqués can be temporarily held in place by touching appliqués with tip of iron. If appliqués are not in desired position, lift and reposition.
5. Fuse appliqués in place.

CROSS STITCH
COUNTED CROSS STITCH (X):

Work one Cross Stitch to correspond to each colored square in chart. For horizontal rows, work stitches in two journeys (Fig. 1).

Fig. 1

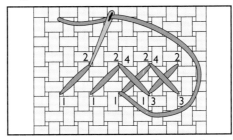

For vertical rows, complete each stitch as shown in Fig. 2.

Fig. 2

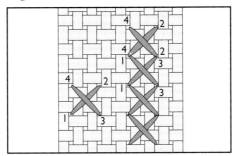

When the chart shows a Backstitch crossing a colored square (Fig. 3), work the Cross Stitch first, then work the Backstitch over the Cross Stitch.

Fig. 3

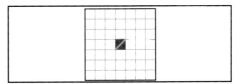

HALF STITCH (½X):

This stitch is one journey of the Cross Stitch and is worked from lower left to upper right (Fig. 4).

Fig. 4

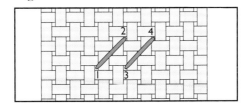

QUARTER STITCH (¼X):

Quarter Stitches are shown as triangular shapes of color in chart and color key. Come up at 1, then split fabric thread to take needle down at 2 (Fig. 5).

Fig. 5

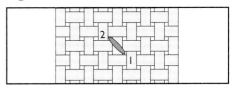

BACKSTITCH (B'ST):

For outline or details, Backstitch (shown in chart and color key by black or colored straight lines) should be worked after all Cross Stitch has been completed (Fig. 6).

Fig. 6

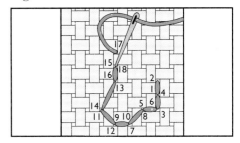

FRENCH KNOT (•)

Referring to Fig. 7, bring needle up at 1. Wrap floss once around needle and insert needle at 2, holding end of floss with non-stitching fingers.

Fig. 7

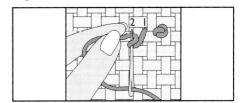

BEADING BASICS
BEADING TIPS
Refer to the project supply list for each project to identify the types of beads and other supplies that we used.

We found that with some types of beads, such as "E" and seed beads, sizes may vary within a package, and the number of beads may need to be adjusted.

Place beads on a paper plate, bowl, or chamois cloth, or use the sticky side of several self-adhesive notes stuck together (to prevent them from curling). To keep from dropping beads, thread beads directly from the plate onto a beading needle.

Pick up several beads on needle before moving them onto the thread. With practice, this is a real time-saver, too.

ADDING BEADS TO FABRIC
Refer to project design and key for bead placement and sew bead in place using a fine needle that will pass through bead. Bring needle up at 1, run needle through bead and then down at 2. Secure thread on back or move to next bead as shown in Fig. 2.

Fig. 1

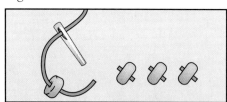

BEADING WITH THREAD
Choose from a variety of beading needles and threads to bead on fabric. We recommend that you work with beading thread, which is stronger than sewing thread. Be sure to use a size needle and thread that will pass through the smallest bead in your project without putting stress on the thread.

Threading Needle
Thread beading needle with one strand of thread unless otherwise indicated in project instructions. It may be helpful to tape the tail to a table as you begin threading beads.

Locking Bead
A locking bead at the beginning of a strand keeps the beads from sliding off your thread. Leaving a 3" tail, string first bead on thread. Pass needle around and through bead again, to lock in place. Thread beads as indicated in project instructions. Locking beads are also used at the end of a thread or dangle.

Securing Thread Ends
To secure an ending thread, lock last bead in place and double back through last four beads; unthread needle, leaving a tail. Add new thread to continue strand (see *Adding Thread*), or trim tail and dot locking bead and thread end with glue; allow to dry.

To secure a beginning thread, rethread needle with beginning tail. Pass needle around locking bead and through next four beads. Trim tail and dot locking bead and thread end with glue; allow to dry.

Adding Thread
To add thread, pass newly threaded needle through the last three beads on the strand, leaving a 3" tail. Thread needle through last bead twice to lock in place and continue beading. Trim tails and dot locking bead and thread ends with glue; allow to dry.

CROCHET TERMINOLOGY	
UNITED STATES	**INTERNATIONAL**
slip stitch (slip st)	= single crochet (sc)
single crochet (sc)	= double crochet (dc)
half double crochet (hdc)	= half treble crochet (htr)
double crochet (dc)	= treble crochet (tr)
treble crochet (tr)	= double treble crochet (dtr)
double treble crochet (dtr)	= triple treble crochet (ttr)
triple treble crochet (tr tr)	= quadruple treble crochet (qtr)
skip	= miss

CROCHET BASICS
CROCHET ABBREVIATIONS
ch(s)	chain(s)
cm	centimeters
dc	double crochet(s)
mm	millimeters

( ) — contains explanatory remarks.
colon (:) — the number(s) given after a colon at the end of a row or round denote(s) the number of stitches or spaces you should have on that row or round.

GAUGE
Exact gauge is **essential** for proper size. Before beginning your Scarf, make the sample swatch given in the individual instructions in the yarn and hook specified. After completing the swatch, measure it, counting your stitches and rows carefully. If your swatch is larger or smaller than specified, **make another, changing hook size to get the correct gauge.** Keep trying until you find the size hook that will give you the specified gauge.

YARN INFORMATION
The Scarf was made with Bulky Weight Yarn and a Medium Weight Novelty "Eyelash" Yarn. Any brand may be used. It is best to refer to the yardage/meters when determining how many balls or skeins to purchase. Remember, to arrive at the finished size, it is the GAUGE/TENSION that is important, not the brand of yarn.

ALUMINUM CROCHET HOOKS	
UNITED STATES	**METRIC (mm)**
B-1	2.25
C-2	2.75
D-3	3.25
E-4	3.5
F-5	3.75
G-6	4
H-8	5
I-9	5.5
J-10	6
K-10½	6.5
N	9
P	10
Q	15

Kitchen Tips

MEASURING INGREDIENTS

Liquid measuring cups have a rim above the measuring line to keep liquid ingredients from spilling. Nested measuring cups are used to measure dry ingredients, butter, shortening, and peanut butter. Measuring spoons are used for measuring both dry and liquid ingredients.

To measure flour or granulated sugar: Spoon ingredient into nested measuring cup and level off with a knife. Do not pack down with spoon.

To measure powdered sugar: Lightly spoon sugar into nested measuring cup and level off with a knife.

To measure brown sugar: Pack sugar into nested measuring cup and level off with a knife. Sugar should hold its shape when removed from cup.

To measure dry ingredients equaling less than $1/4$ cup: Dip measuring spoon into ingredient and level off with a knife.

To measure butter, shortening, or peanut butter: Pack ingredient firmly into nested measuring cup and level off with a knife.

To measure liquids: Use a liquid measuring cup placed on a flat surface. Pour ingredient into cup and check measuring line at eye level.

To measure honey or syrup: For a more accurate measurement, lightly spray measuring cup or spoon with vegetable oil cooking spray before measuring so the liquid will release easily from cup or spoon.

WHIPPING CREAM

For greatest volume, beat whipping cream in a chilled glass bowl with chilled beaters until soft peaks form. In warm weather, place chilled bowl over ice while beating cream.

EQUIVALENT MEASUREMENTS

1 tablespoon	=	3 teaspoons
$1/8$ cup (1 fluid ounce)	=	2 tablespoons
$1/4$ cup (2 fluid ounces)	=	4 tablespoons
$1/3$ cup	=	$5^1/3$ tablespoons
$1/2$ cup (4 fluid ounces)	=	8 tablespoons
$3/4$ cup (6 fluid ounces)	=	12 tablespoons
1 cup (8 fluid ounces)	=	16 tablespoons or $1/2$ pint
2 cups (16 fluid ounces)	=	1 pint
1 quart (32 fluid ounces)	=	2 pints
$1/2$ gallon (64 fluid ounces)	=	2 quarts
1 gallon (128 fluid ounces)	=	4 quarts

HELPFUL FOOD EQUIVALENTS

$1/2$ cup butter	=	1 stick butter
1 square baking chocolate	=	1 ounce chocolate
1 cup chocolate chips	=	6 ounces chocolate chips
$2^1/4$ cups packed brown sugar	=	1 pound brown sugar
$3^1/2$ cups unsifted powdered sugar	=	1 pound powdered sugar
2 cups granulated sugar	=	1 pound granulated sugar
4 cups sifted all-purpose flour	=	1 pound all-purpose flour
1 cup shredded cheese	=	4 ounces cheese
3 cups sliced carrots	=	1 pound carrots
$1/2$ cup chopped celery	=	1 rib celery
$1/2$ cup chopped onion	=	1 medium onion
1 cup chopped green pepper	=	1 large green pepper

Project Index

Recipe Index

Credits

We want to extend a warm thank you to the generous people who allowed us to photograph our projects at their homes.

Radiant Stars and Updated Classics: Nancy Appleton
Christmas is for Children: Rhonda Fitz
A Splendid Evening: Brenda and Kerry Snyder
A Season of Serenity: Christy Myers
Ranch Hand Roundup: Tom and Alison Melson
Gifts from Hand to Heart: Morgan Hall
Holiday Cooking Club: Price and Joy Kloess; Donald and Susan Huff

Our sincere appreciation goes to Jerry Davis Photography, Mark Mathews Photography, Larry Pennington of Pennington Studios, and Ken West Photography, all of Little Rock, Arkansas, for their excellent photography. Photography stylists Sondra Harrison Daniel, Karen Smart Hall, and Christy Myers also deserve a special mention for the high quality of their collaboration with these photographers.

We would like to recognize Husqvarna Viking Sewing Machine Company of Cleveland, Ohio, for providing the sewing machines used to make many of our projects, and Royal Langnickel for the paintbrushes used on all painted designs.

We are sincerely grateful to Belinda Baxter, Jeni Boyd, and Karla Edgar, who helped craft several of our projects.